National Vital Statistics Reports

From the CENTERS FOR DISEASE CONTROL AND PREVENTION
National Center for Health Statistics
National Vital Statistics System

I0415824

Volume 48, Number 18

February 7, 2001

United States Life Tables, 1998

by Robert N. Anderson, Ph.D., Division of Vital Statistics

> Figure 3 has been revised from the printed copy.

Abstract

The life tables in this report are current life tables for the United States based on age-specific death rates in 1998. Data used to prepare these life tables are 1998 final mortality statistics; July 1, 1998, population estimates; and data from the Medicare program. Presented are complete life tables by age, race, and sex. In 1998 the overall expectation of life at birth was 76.7 years, an increase of 0.2 years compared with life expectancy in 1997. Life expectancy increased from 1997 to 1998 for each of the four race-sex groups for which life expectancy is reported. Life expectancy increased for black males by 0.4 year (from 67.2 to 67.6), for black females by 0.1 year (from 74.7 to 74.8), for white males by 0.2 year (from 74.3 to 74.5), and for white females by 0.1 year (from 79.9 to 80.0).

Introduction

Death rates for a specific period may be summarized by the life table method to obtain measures of comparative longevity. There are two types of life tables—the generation or cohort life table and the current life table.

The generation life table provides a "longitudinal" perspective in that it follows the mortality experience of a particular cohort, all persons born in the year 1900, for example, from the moment of birth through consecutive ages in successive calendar years. Based on age-specific death rates observed through consecutive calendar years, the generation life table reflects the mortality experience of an actual cohort from birth until no lives remain in the group. To prepare just a single complete generation life table requires data over many years. It is not feasible to construct generation life tables entirely on the basis of actual data for cohorts (1). It is necessary to project data for the incomplete period for cohorts whose life spans are not yet complete (2).

The better-known current life table may, in contrast, be characterized as "cross-sectional." Unlike the generation life table, the current life table does not represent the mortality experience of an actual cohort. Rather, the current life table considers a hypothetical cohort and assumes that it is subject to the age-specific death rates observed for an actual population during a particular period. Thus, for example, a current life table for 1998 assumes a hypothetical cohort subject throughout its lifetime to the age-specific death rates prevailing for the actual population in 1998. The current life table may thus be characterized as rendering a "snapshot" of current mortality experience, and shows the long-range implications of a set of age-specific death rates that prevailed in a given year. In this report the term "life table" refers only to the current life table and not to the generation life table.

Data and methods

The data used to prepare the U.S. life tables for 1998 are final mortality statistics for 1998; July 1, 1998, population estimates prepared by the U.S. Bureau of the Census; and data from the Medicare program prepared by the Health Care Financing Administration. Data from the Medicare program are used to calculate probabilities of dying for ages over 85 years (see Technical notes).

Life tables can be classified in two ways according to the length of the age interval in which data are presented. A complete life table contains data for every single year of age. An abridged life table typically contains data by 5- or 10-year age intervals. A complete life table, of course, can be easily aggregated into 5- or 10-year age groups (see Technical notes for instructions on how to do this). U.S. life tables based on data prior to 1997 other than the decennial life tables are abridged life tables constructed by reference to a "standard" table (3). The 1998 U.S. life tables are complete life tables calculated using a method implemented with the 1997 life tables and similar to that of the U.S. Decennial Life Tables (4, 5). See Technical notes for more information on the method used to construct the life tables in this report.

Acknowledgments

This report was prepared in the Division of Vital Statistics under the general direction of Harry M. Rosenberg, Chief of the Mortality Statistics Branch. Registration Methods staff and the Data Acquisition and Evaluation Branch provided consultation to State vital statistics offices regarding the collection of the death certificate data on which this report is based. This report was edited by Demarius V. Miller, typeset by Jacqueline M. Davis, and graphics were produced by Jarmila Ogburn of the Publications Branch, Division of Data Services.

Expectation of life—The most frequently used life table statistic is life expectancy (e_x), which is the average number of years of life remaining for persons who have attained a given age (x). Life expectancy and other life table values for each age in 1998 are shown for the total population and by race and sex in tables 1–9. Life expectancy is summarized by age, race, and sex in table A.

Life expectancy at birth (e_0) for 1998 for the total population was 76.7 years. This represents the average number of years that the members of the life table cohort may expect to live at the time of birth (table A).

Survivors to specified ages—Another way of assessing the longevity of the life table cohort is by determining the proportion who survive to specified ages. The l_x column of the life table provides the data for computing the proportion. Table B summarizes the number of survivors by age, race, and sex. To illustrate, 81,931 persons out of the original 1998 life table cohort of 100,000 (or 81.9 percent) were alive at exact age 65. In other words, the probability that a person will survive from birth to age 65, given 1998 age-specific mortality, is 81.9 percent. Probabilities of survival can be calculated at any age by simply dividing the number of survivors at the terminal age by the number at the beginning age. For example, to calculate the probability of surviving from age 20 to age 85, one would divide the number of survivors at age 85 (34,537) by the number of survivors at age 20 (98,595), which results in a 35.0 percent probability of survival.

Explanation of the columns of the life table

Column 1—Age (x to x + 1)—This column shows the age interval between the two exact ages indicated. For instance, "20–21" means the 1-year interval between the 20th and 21st birthdays.

Column 2—Proportion dying (q_x)—This column shows the proportion of the cohort who are alive at the beginning of an indicated age interval and who will die before reaching the end of that age interval. For example, for males in the age interval 20–21 years, the proportion dying is 0.00131 (table 2). Out of every 100,000 males alive and exactly

20 years of age at the beginning of the period, 131 will die before reaching their 21st birthday. The "proportion dying" column forms the basis of the life table. The life table is so constructed that all other columns are derived from it.

Column 3—Number surviving (l_x)—This column shows the number of persons, starting with a cohort of 100,000 live births, who survive to the exact age marking the beginning of each age interval. The l_x values are computed from the q_x values, which are successively applied to the remainder of the original 100,000 persons still alive at the beginning of each age interval. Thus out of 100,000 female babies born alive, 99,345 will complete the first year of life and enter the second; 99,144 will reach age 10; 98,857 will reach age 20; and 42,297 will live to age 85 (table 3).

Column 4—Number dying (d_x)—This column shows the number dying in each successive age interval out of 100,000 live births. Out of 100,000 males born alive, 785 will die in the first year of life; 129 in the between ages 20 and 21; and 757 will die after reaching age 100 (table 2). Each figure in column 4 is the difference between two successive figures in column 3.

Columns 5 and 6—Stationary population $(L_x$ and $T_x)$—Suppose that a group of 100,000 individuals like that assumed in columns 3 and 4 is born every year and that the proportions dying in each such group in each age interval throughout the lives of the members are exactly those shown in column 2. If there were no migration and if the births were evenly distributed over the calendar year, the survivors of these births would make up what is called a stationary population—stationary because in such a population the number of persons living in any given age group would never change. When individuals left the group, either by death or by growing older and entering the next higher age group, their places would immediately be taken by persons entering from the next lower age group. Thus, a census taken at any time in such a stationary community would always show the same total population and the same numerical distribution of that population among the various age groups. In such a stationary population supported by 100,000 annual births, column 3 shows the number of persons who, each year,

Table A. Expectation of life by age, race, and sex: United States, 1998

Age	All races			White			Black		
	Total	Male	Female	Total	Male	Female	Total	Male	Female
0	76.7	73.8	79.5	77.3	74.5	80.0	71.3	67.6	74.8
1	76.3	73.4	79.0	76.8	74.0	79.4	71.4	67.7	74.8
5	72.4	69.5	75.1	72.9	70.1	75.5	67.6	63.9	70.9
10	67.4	64.6	70.2	67.9	65.2	70.6	62.6	59.0	66.0
15	62.5	59.7	65.2	63.0	60.2	65.6	57.7	54.1	61.1
20	57.7	55.0	60.3	58.2	55.5	60.8	53.0	49.5	56.2
25	53.0	50.3	55.5	53.4	50.8	55.9	48.4	45.1	51.4
30	48.2	45.7	50.6	48.6	46.1	51.0	43.8	40.6	46.7
35	43.5	41.0	45.8	43.9	41.5	46.2	39.3	36.2	42.0
40	38.8	36.4	41.1	39.2	36.8	41.4	34.9	31.9	37.5
45	34.3	31.9	36.4	34.6	32.3	36.7	30.6	27.7	33.1
50	29.8	27.6	31.8	30.1	27.9	32.0	26.6	23.9	28.8
55	25.5	23.5	27.4	25.7	23.7	27.6	22.8	20.4	24.8
60	21.5	19.6	23.2	21.6	19.7	23.3	19.3	17.1	21.0
65	17.8	16.0	19.2	17.8	16.1	19.3	16.1	14.3	17.4
70	14.3	12.8	15.5	14.4	12.8	15.6	13.0	11.5	14.1
75	11.3	10.0	12.2	11.3	10.0	12.2	10.5	9.2	11.3
80	8.6	7.5	9.2	8.5	7.5	9.1	8.2	7.1	8.7
85	6.3	5.5	6.7	6.3	5.4	6.6	6.3	5.5	6.6
90	4.7	4.1	4.9	4.5	4.0	4.7	4.8	4.3	4.9
95	3.5	3.0	3.6	3.3	2.9	3.4	3.7	3.4	3.7
100	2.6	2.3	2.7	2.4	2.2	2.4	2.8	2.7	2.8

Table B. Number of survivors by age, out of 100,000 born alive, by race and sex: United States, 1998

Age	All races			White			Black		
	Total	Male	Female	Total	Male	Female	Total	Male	Female
0	100,000	100,000	100,000	100,000	100,000	100,000	100,000	100,000	100,000
1	99,279	99,215	99,345	99,404	99,352	99,458	98,566	98,421	98,715
5	99,141	99,066	99,220	99,284	99,222	99,348	98,323	98,149	98,503
10	99,053	98,967	99,144	99,206	99,134	99,281	98,180	97,986	98,380
15	98,944	98,834	99,059	99,103	99,012	99,199	98,033	97,799	98,276
20	98,595	98,346	98,857	98,773	98,563	98,995	97,556	97,068	98,063
25	98,126	97,648	98,627	98,354	97,942	98,791	96,775	95,867	97,697
30	97,648	96,970	98,350	97,936	97,348	98,553	95,904	94,609	97,187
35	97,062	96,184	97,964	97,418	96,646	98,221	94,846	93,203	96,445
40	96,267	95,163	97,398	96,707	95,722	97,731	93,403	91,396	95,336
45	95,135	93,717	96,582	95,698	94,414	97,027	91,293	88,757	93,710
50	93,491	91,616	95,392	94,228	92,528	95,981	88,174	84,731	91,399
55	91,094	88,646	93,562	92,021	89,800	94,298	83,958	79,315	88,241
60	87,442	84,188	90,700	88,582	85,600	91,616	78,210	72,158	83,723
65	81,931	77,547	86,288	83,280	79,211	87,390	70,516	62,829	77,480
70	74,199	68,375	79,926	75,618	70,065	81,151	61,604	52,886	69,589
75	63,634	56,288	70,761	65,079	57,899	72,110	49,915	40,667	58,464
80	50,523	42,127	58,573	51,807	43,462	59,852	37,463	28,375	45,963
85	34,537	26,219	42,297	35,463	27,058	43,316	24,189	16,434	31,388
90	18,614	12,310	24,214	19,055	12,620	24,761	12,647	7,494	17,328
95	7,166	3,910	9,911	7,160	3,881	9,906	4,995	2,546	7,123
100	1,761	757	2,594	1,609	681	2,361	1,351	607	1,952

reach the birthday that marks the beginning of the age interval indicated in column 1, and column 4 shows the number of persons who die each year in the indicated age interval.

Column 5 shows the number of persons in the stationary population in the indicated age interval. For example, the figure given for females in the age interval 20–21 years is 98,835 (table 3). This means that in a stationary population of males supported by 100,000 annual births and with proportions dying in each age group always in accordance with column 2, a census taken on any date would show 98,835 persons between exact ages 20 and 21 years. This figure also represents the average number of person-years of exposure to the risk of dying during the age interval 20–21 years.

Column 6 shows the total number of persons in the stationary population (column 5) in the indicated age interval and all subsequent age intervals. For example, in the stationary population of females referred to in the last illustration, column 6 shows that there would be at any given moment a total of 5,964,918 persons who have passed their 20th birthday (table 3). The female population at all ages 0 and above (the total female population of the stationary community) would be 7,947,682.

Column 7—Average remaining lifetime (e$_x$)—The average remaining lifetime (also called life expectancy) at any given age is the average number of years remaining to be lived by those surviving to that age on the basis of a given set of age-specific rates of dying. To arrive at this value, it is first necessary to observe that the figures in column 5 of the life table can also be interpreted in terms of a single life table cohort without introducing the concept of the stationary population. From this point of view, each figure in column 5 represents the total time (in years) lived between two indicated birthdays by all those reaching the earlier birthday. Thus, the figure 98,282 (column 5) for males in the age interval 20–21 is the total number of years lived between the 20th and 21st birthdays by the 98,346 (column 3) males who reached their 20th birthday out of 100,000 males born alive (table 2). The corresponding figure 5,404,334 in column 6 is the total

number of years lived after attaining age 20 by the 98,346 reaching that age. The former figure divided by the latter (5,404,334 divided by 98,346) gives 55.0 years as the average remaining lifetime of males at age 20.

Results

Life expectancy in the United States

Tables 1–9 show complete life tables by race (white and black) and sex for 1998. Tables A and B summarize life expectancy and survival by age, race, and sex. Life expectancy at birth for 1998 represents the average number of years that a group of infants would live if the infants were to experience throughout life the age-specific death rates prevailing in 1998. In 1998 life expectancy at birth was 76.7 years, an increase of 0.2 year compared with life expectancy in 1997 and represents a record high for life expectancy in the United States. The increase between 1997 and 1998 represents the continuation of the general upward trend in U.S. life expectancy observed throughout the 20th century (6).

In 1998 life expectancy for females was 79.5 years, an increase of 0.1 year from 1997. Life expectancy was 73.8 years for males, a 0.2-year increase from 1997 to 1998. The difference in life expectancy between the sexes was 5.7 years in 1998, a very slight narrowing from the difference (5.8) in the previous year. From 1900 to 1975, the difference in life expectancy between the sexes increased from 2.8 years to 7.8 years. The increasing gap during these years is attributed to increases in male mortality due to ischemic heart disease and lung cancer, both of which increased largely as the result of men's early and widespread adoption of cigarette smoking (6, 7). Since 1979, the difference in life expectancy between the sexes has narrowed from 7.8 years to 5.7 years, reflecting proportionately greater increases in lung cancer mortality for women than for men and proportionately larger decreases in heart disease mortality among men (6, 7).

Between 1997 and 1998, life expectancy for the black population rose 0.2 year to 71.3 years. For the white population it increased 0.1 year from 77.2 years to 77.3 years. The difference in life expectancy between the white and black populations was 6.0 years in 1998, a slight narrowing of the gap from 1997 (6.1 years). Although the white-black difference in life expectancy narrowed from 15.8 years in 1900 to 5.7 years in 1982, it increased to 7.1 years in 1993 before declining from 1994 (7.0 years) to 1998 (6.0 years). The increase in the gap from 1983 to 1993 was largely the result of increases in mortality among the black male population due to HIV infection and homicide (6, 8).

Among the four race-sex groups (figure 1), white females continued to have the highest life expectancy at birth (80.0 years), followed by black females (74.8 years), white males (74.5 years), and black males (67.6 years). Between 1997 and 1998, life expectancy increased 0.4 year for black males (from 67.2 in 1997 to 67.6 in 1998). Black males experienced an unprecedented decline in life expectancy every year for 1984–89 (8), but annual increases in 1990–92 and 1994–98. From 1997 to 1998, life expectancy for black females rose from 74.7 years to 74.8 years, an increase of 0.1 year. Life expectancy for white males rose 0.2 year, from 74.3 years in 1997 to 74.5 years in 1998. White female life expectancy increased during the same period by 0.1 year from 79.9 years to 80.0 years. Overall, the largest gains in life expectancy between 1980 and 1997 were for white and black males (3.8 years for both groups), black females (2.3 years), and white females (1.9 years) (table 12).

The 1998 life table may be used to compare life expectancies at any age from birth onward. On the basis of mortality experienced in 1998, a person aged 65 years could expect to live an average of 17.8 more years for a total of 82.8 years, and a person aged 100 years could expect to live an additional 2.6 years on average (table A). Life expect-ancy at 100 years of age, particularly for the black population, should be interpreted with caution as these figures may be affected somewhat by age misreporting (4, 9, 10).

Survivorship in the United States

Table B summarizes the number of survivors out of 100,000 persons born alive (l_x) by age, race, and sex. Table 10 shows trends in survivorship from 1900 to 1998. In 1998, 99.3 percent of all infants born in the United States survived the first year of life. In contrast, only 87.6 percent of infants born in 1900 survived the first year. About one-half of the 1998 cohort survived to age 80, the median age at death, and about 1.8 percent survived to age 100. In 1900 the median age at death was 58 and only 0.03 percent survived to age 100.

Among the four race-sex groups (figure 2 and table B), white females have the highest median age at death with 50 percent surviving to age 83. Of the original hypothetical cohort of 100,000 infant white females, 99.0 percent survive to age 20, 87.4 percent survive to age 65, and 43.3 percent survive to age 85. For white males and black females, the pattern of survival by age is similar. These groups have approxi-mately the same median age at death of 78 years. However, white males have slightly higher survival rates than black females at the younger ages with 98.6 percent surviving to age 20 and 79.2 percent surviving to age 65 compared with 98.1 percent and 77.5 percent, respectively, for black females. At the older ages, in contrast, black female survival surpasses white male survival. At age 85, white male survival is 27.1 percent compared with 31.4 percent for black females. This cross-over, which occurs at about age 72, is clearly shown in figure 2. The median age at death for black males is 71 years, 12 years less than that for white females; 97.1 percent of black males survive to age 20, 62.8 percent to age 65, and 16.4 percent to age 85. By age 100, there is very little difference between the white and black populations in terms of survival. Somewhat less than 1 percent of white and black males and about 2 percent of white and black females survive to age 100.

Plotting the percent surviving by age for the periods 1900–1902, 1949–51, and 1998 shows an increasingly "rectangular" survival curve (figure 3). That is, the survival curve has become increasingly flat in response to progressively lower mortality, particularly at the younger ages, and increasingly vertical at the older ages. The survival curve for 1900–1902 shows a rapid decline in survival in the first few years of life and a relatively steady decline thereafter. In contrast, the survival curve for 1998 is nearly flat until about age 50 after which the decline in survival becomes more rapid. Improvements in survival between 1900–1902 and 1949–51 occurred at all ages, although the largest improvements were among the younger population. Between 1949–51 and 1998, improvements occurred primarily for the older population.

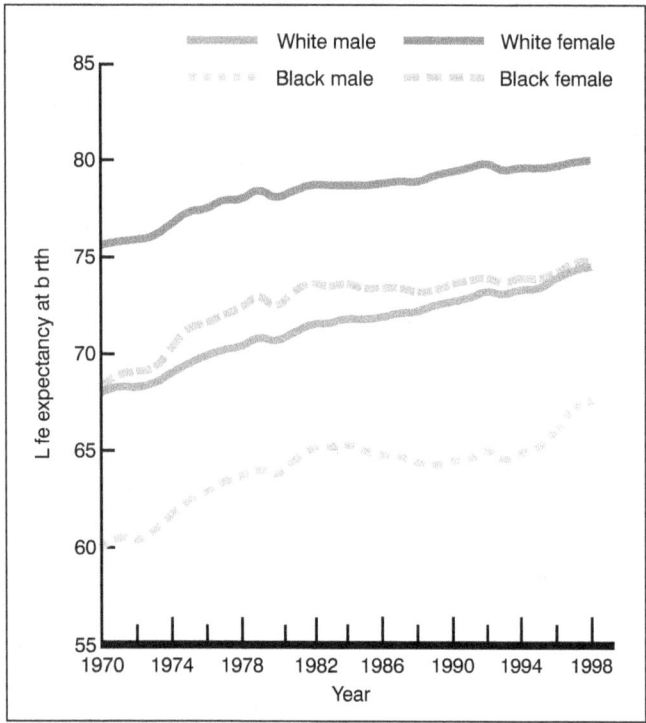

Figure 1. Life expectancy at birth by race and sex: 1970–98

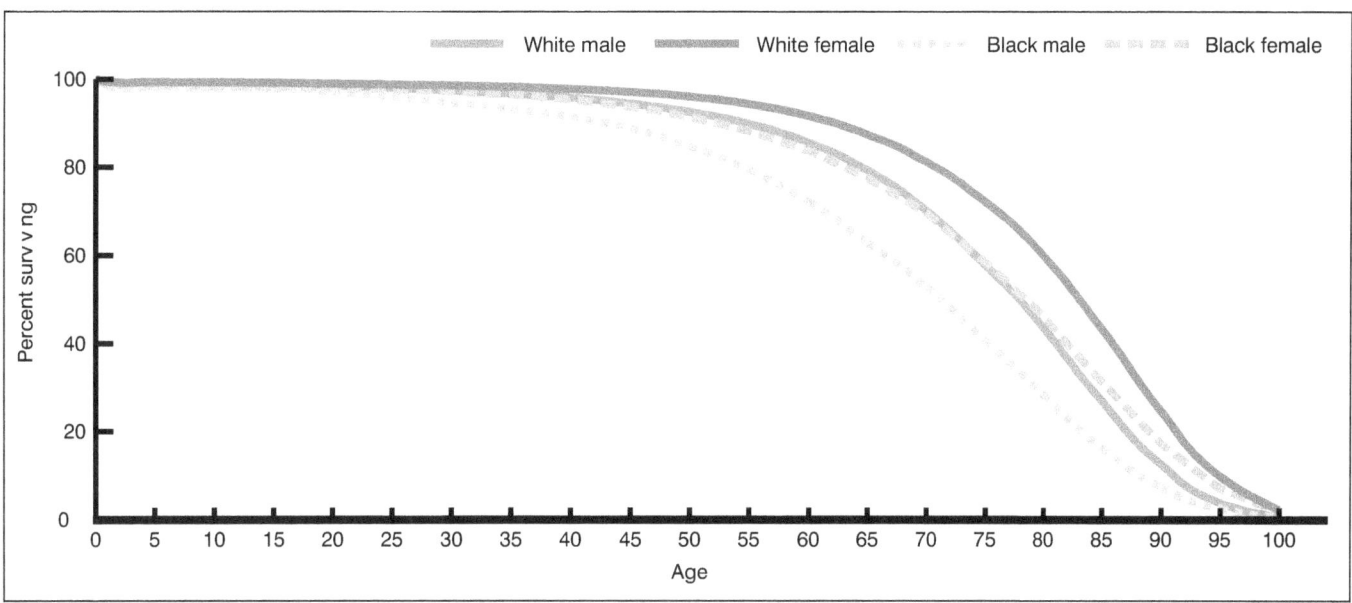

Figure 2. Percent surviving by age, race, and sex: United States, 1998

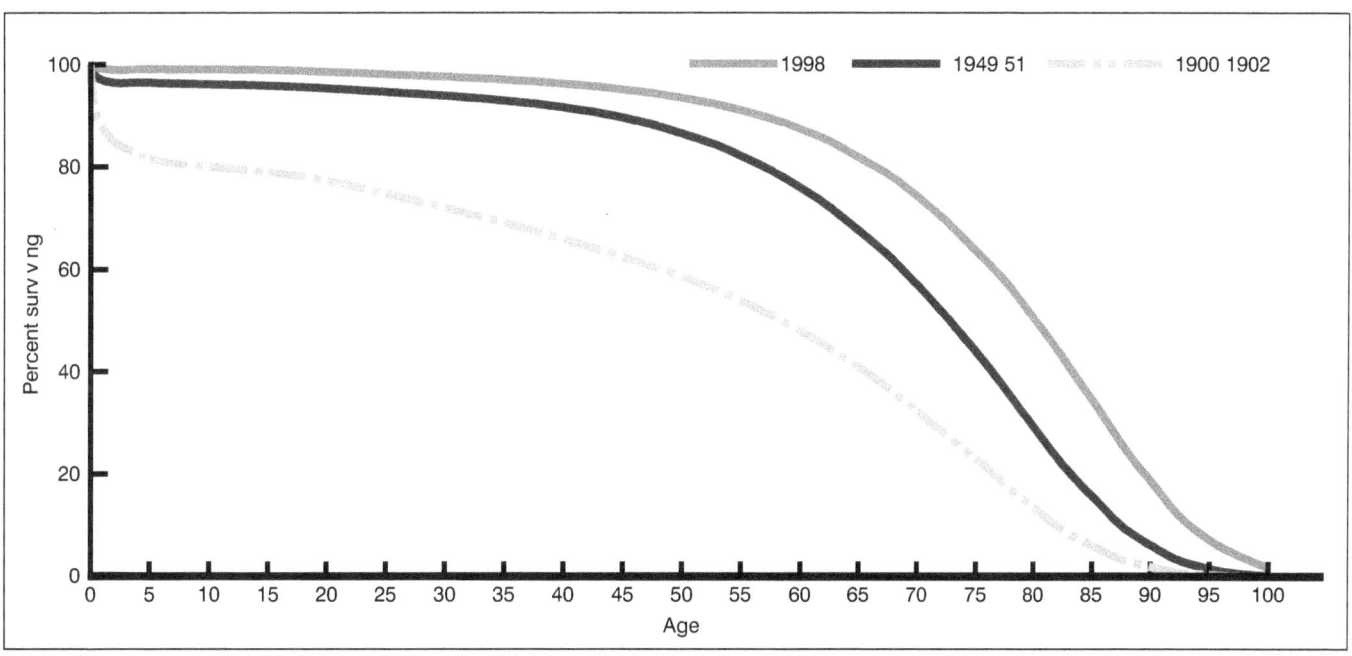

Figure 3. Percent surviving by age: Death-registration States, 1900–1902, and United States, 1949–51 and 1998

References

1. Shryock HS, Siegel JS, et al. The methods and materials of demography, vol 2. U.S. Bureau of the Census. Washington: U.S. Government Printing Office. 1971.

2. Moriyama IM, Gustavus SO. Cohort mortality and survivorship, United States death-registration States, 1900–68. National Center for Health Statistics. Vital Health Stat 3(16). 1972.

3. Sirken MG. Comparison of two methods of constructing abridged life tables by reference to a "standard" table. National Center for Health Statistics. Vital Health Stat 2(4). 1966.

4. Anderson RN. A method for constructing complete annual U.S. life tables. National Center for Health Statistics. Vital Health Stat 2(129). 1999.

5. Armstrong RJ. Methodology of the national and State life tables. U.S. decennial life tables for 1989–91 vol 1 no 2. Hyattsville, Maryland: National Center for Health Statistics. 1998.

6. Anderson RN. Some trends and comparisons of United States life table data: 1900–91. U.S. decennial life tables for 1989–91 vol 1 no 3. Hyattsville, Maryland: National Center for Health Statistics. 1999.

7. Waldron I. Recent trends in sex mortality ratios for adults in developed countries. Social Science and Medicine 36:451–62. 1993.

8. Kochanek KD, Maurer JD, Rosenberg HM. Causes of death contributing to changes in life expectancy: United States, 1984–89. National Center for Health Statistics. Vital Health Stat 20(23). 1994.

9. Kestenbaum B. A description of the extreme aged population based on improved Medicare enrollment data. Demography. 29:565–80. 1992.

10. Coale AJ, Kisker EE. Defects in data on old-age mortality in the United States: New procedures for calculating mortality schedules and life tables at the highest ages. Asian and Pacific Population Forum. 4:1–31. 1990.

11. Greville TNE, Carlson GA. Estimated average length of life in the death-registration States. National Center for Health Statistics. Vital statistics—special reports. Vol 33 no 9. Washington: Public Health Service. 1951.

12. U.S. Bureau of the Census. U.S. population estimates, by age, race, sex, and Hispanic origin: 1996. Census file RES0796. 1997.

13. U.S. Bureau of the Census. Age, sex, race, and Hispanic origin information from the 1990 Census: A comparison of census results where age and race have been modified. 1990 CPH-1-74. Washington: U.S. Department of Commerce. 1991.

14. Kestenbaum B. Recent mortality of the oldest old, from Medicare data. Paper presented at the 1997 meetings of the Population Association of America, March 27–29. 1997.

15. Horiuchi S, Wilmoth JR. Deceleration in the age pattern of mortality at older ages. Demography. 35:391–412. 1998.

16. Wilmoth JR. Are mortality rates falling at extremely high ages? An investigation based on a model proposed by Coale and Kisker. Population Studies. 49:281–95. 1995.

17. Murphy SL. Deaths: Final data for 1998. National Vital Statistics Reports; vol 48 no 11. Hyattsville, Maryland: National Center for Health Statistics. 2000.

List of detailed tables

1. Life table for the total population: United States, 1998   7
2. Life table for males: United States, 1998   9
3. Life table for females: United States, 1998   11
4. Life table for the white population: United States, 1998   13
5. Life table for white males: United States, 1998   15
6. Life table for white females: United States, 1998   17
7. Life table for the black population: United States, 1998   19
8. Life table for black males: United States, 1998   21
9. Life table for black females: United States, 1998   23
10. Survivorship by age, race, and sex: Death-registration States, 1900–1902 to 1919–21, and United States, 1929–31 to 1998   25
11. Life expectancy by age, race, and sex: Death-registration States, 1900–1902 to 1919–21, and United States, 1929–31 to 1998   29
12. Estimated life expectancy at birth in years, by race and sex: Death-registration States, 1900–28, and United States, 1929–98   33

Table 1. Life table for the total population: United States, 1998

Age	Proportion dying during age interval q_x	Number living at beginning of age interval l_x	Number dying during age interval d_x	Stationary population in the age interval L_x	Stationary population in this and all subsequent age intervals T_x	Life expectancy at beginning of age interval e_x
0–1.	0.00721	100,000	721	99,370	7,671,400	76.7
1–2.	0.00055	99,279	54	99,252	7,572,030	76.3
2–3.	0.00036	99,225	36	99,207	7,472,779	75.3
3–4.	0.00026	99,189	26	99,176	7,373,572	74.3
4–5.	0.00021	99,162	21	99,152	7,274,396	73.4
5–6.	0.00020	99,141	20	99,131	7,175,244	72.4
6–7.	0.00019	99,121	19	99,112	7,076,113	71.4
7–8.	0.00018	99,102	18	99,094	6,977,001	70.4
8–9.	0.00017	99,085	16	99,076	6,877,908	69.4
9–10.	0.00015	99,068	15	99,061	6,778,831	68.4
10–11.	0.00013	99,053	13	99,047	6,679,771	67.4
11–12.	0.00014	99,040	14	99,033	6,580,724	66.4
12–13.	0.00018	99,027	18	99,018	6,481,690	65.5
13–14.	0.00027	99,009	27	98,995	6,382,673	64.5
14–15.	0.00039	98,982	38	98,963	6,283,677	63.5
15–16.	0.00052	98,944	51	98,918	6,184,714	62.5
16–17.	0.00064	98,893	63	98,861	6,085,796	61.5
17–18.	0.00073	98,830	72	98,793	5,986,935	60.6
18–19.	0.00080	98,757	79	98,718	5,888,142	59.6
19–20.	0.00085	98,678	83	98,636	5,789,424	58.7
20–21.	0.00089	98,595	88	98,551	5,690,788	57.7
21–22.	0.00094	98,507	93	98,460	5,592,237	56.8
22–23.	0.00097	98,414	96	98,366	5,493,777	55.8
23–24.	0.00098	98,318	97	98,270	5,395,411	54.9
24–25.	0.00097	98,221	96	98,174	5,297,141	53.9
25–26.	0.00096	98,126	94	98,079	5,198,968	53.0
26–27.	0.00095	98,032	93	97,985	5,100,889	52.0
27–28.	0.00096	97,938	94	97,891	5,002,904	51.1
28–29.	0.00098	97,845	96	97,796	4,905,013	50.1
29–30.	0.00103	97,748	100	97,698	4,807,216	49.2
30–31.	0.00108	97,648	105	97,595	4,709,518	48.2
31–32.	0.00113	97,543	110	97,488	4,611,923	47.3
32–33.	0.00119	97,433	116	97,375	4,514,435	46.3
33–34.	0.00127	97,317	123	97,255	4,417,060	45.4
34–35.	0.00135	97,193	131	97,128	4,319,805	44.4
35–36.	0.00144	97,062	139	96,992	4,222,678	43.5
36–37.	0.00153	96,923	148	96,849	4,125,686	42.6
37–38.	0.00163	96,775	157	96,696	4,028,837	41.6
38–39.	0.00174	96,617	169	96,533	3,932,141	40.7
39–40.	0.00188	96,449	181	96,358	3,835,608	39.8
40–41.	0.00203	96,267	195	96,170	3,739,250	38.8
41–42.	0.00218	96,072	210	95,968	3,643,080	37.9
42–43.	0.00235	95,863	225	95,750	3,547,113	37.0
43–44.	0.00253	95,638	242	95,517	3,451,363	36.1
44–45.	0.00273	95,396	260	95,266	3,355,846	35.2
45–46.	0.00295	95,135	281	94,995	3,260,580	34.3
46–47.	0.00320	94,855	304	94,703	3,165,585	33.4
47–48.	0.00347	94,551	328	94,387	3,070,883	32.5
48–49.	0.00375	94,223	353	94,046	2,976,496	31.6
49–50.	0.00404	93,870	379	93,680	2,882,449	30.7
50–51.	0.00436	93,491	408	93,287	2,788,769	29.8
51–52.	0.00473	93,083	440	92,863	2,695,482	29.0
52–53.	0.00513	92,643	475	92,405	2,602,619	28.1
53–54.	0.00558	92,168	515	91,910	2,510,214	27.2
54–55.	0.00610	91,653	559	91,374	2,418,304	26.4
55–56.	0.00669	91,094	609	90,790	2,326,930	25.5
56–57.	0.00736	90,485	666	90,152	2,236,140	24.7
57–58.	0.00809	89,819	727	89,456	2,145,988	23.9
58–59.	0.00888	89,093	791	88,697	2,056,532	23.1
59–60.	0.00973	88,301	859	87,871	1,967,835	22.3
60–61.	0.01068	87,442	934	86,975	1,879,964	21.5
61–62.	0.01174	86,508	1,016	86,000	1,792,989	20.7
62–63.	0.01288	85,492	1,102	84,941	1,706,989	20.0
63–64.	0.01407	84,390	1,187	83,797	1,622,048	19.2
64–65.	0.01529	83,203	1,272	82,567	1,538,251	18.5
65–66.	0.01651	81,931	1,353	81,254	1,455,684	17.8
66–67.	0.01781	80,578	1,435	79,860	1,374,430	17.1

Table 1. Life table for the total population: United States, 1998—Con.

Age	Proportion dying during age interval q_x	Number living at beginning of age interval l_x	Number dying during age interval d_x	Stationary population in the age interval L_x	Stationary population in this and all subsequent age intervals T_x	Life expectancy at beginning of age interval e_x
67–68	0.01934	79,142	1,531	78,377	1,294,570	16.4
68–69	0.02118	77,612	1,644	76,790	1,216,193	15.7
69–70	0.02328	75,968	1,769	75,083	1,139,403	15.0
70–71	0.02551	74,199	1,893	73,252	1,064,320	14.3
71–72	0.02777	72,306	2,008	71,302	991,067	13.7
72–73	0.03012	70,298	2,118	69,240	919,765	13.1
73–74	0.03260	68,181	2,223	67,069	850,526	12.5
74–75	0.03523	65,958	2,324	64,796	783,456	11.9
75–76	0.03799	63,634	2,418	62,425	718,660	11.3
76–77	0.04096	61,216	2,508	59,963	656,235	10.7
77–78	0.04440	58,709	2,607	57,405	596,272	10.2
78–79	0.04855	56,102	2,724	54,740	538,867	9.6
79–80	0.05349	53,378	2,855	51,951	484,127	9.1
80–81	0.05923	50,523	2,993	49,027	432,176	8.6
81–82	0.06566	47,530	3,121	45,970	383,149	8.1
82–83	0.07272	44,410	3,230	42,795	337,179	7.6
83–84	0.08022	41,180	3,304	39,528	294,384	7.1
84–85	0.08818	37,876	3,340	36,207	254,856	6.7
85–86	0.09673	34,537	3,341	32,866	218,650	6.3
86–87	0.10587	31,196	3,303	29,544	185,783	6.0
87–88	0.11558	27,893	3,224	26,281	156,239	5.6
88–89	0.12589	24,669	3,106	23,116	129,958	5.3
89–90	0.13680	21,563	2,950	20,089	106,841	5.0
90–91	0.14830	18,614	2,760	17,233	86,753	4.7
91–92	0.16038	15,853	2,542	14,582	69,519	4.4
92–93	0.17303	13,311	2,303	12,159	54,937	4.1
93–94	0.18623	11,008	2,050	9,983	42,778	3.9
94–95	0.19997	8,958	1,791	8,062	32,795	3.7
95–96	0.21421	7,166	1,535	6,399	24,733	3.5
96–97	0.22892	5,631	1,289	4,987	18,334	3.3
97–98	0.24406	4,342	1,060	3,812	13,348	3.1
98–99	0.25957	3,282	852	2,856	9,535	2.9
99–100	0.27542	2,430	669	2,096	6,679	2.7
100+	1.00000	1,761	1,761	4,583	4,583	2.6

Table 2. Life table for males: United States, 1998

Age	Proportion dying during age interval q_x	Number living at beginning of age interval l_x	Number dying during age interval d_x	Stationary population in the age interval L_x	Stationary population in this and all subsequent age intervals T_x	Life expectancy at beginning of age interval e_x
0–1	0.00785	100,000	785	99,316	7,382,896	73.8
1–2	0.00058	99,215	57	99,187	7,283,580	73.4
2–3	0.00040	99,158	40	99,138	7,184,394	72.5
3–4	0.00029	99,118	29	99,104	7,085,256	71.5
4–5	0.00024	99,089	24	99,078	6,986,152	70.5
5–6	0.00022	99,066	22	99,055	6,887,074	69.5
6–7	0.00022	99,044	21	99,033	6,788,019	68.5
7–8	0.00021	99,022	21	99,012	6,688,986	67.6
8–9	0.00019	99,002	19	98,992	6,589,974	66.6
9–10	0.00016	98,983	16	98,975	6,490,982	65.6
10–11	0.00014	98,967	14	98,960	6,392,007	64.6
11–12	0.00015	98,953	14	98,946	6,293,047	63.6
12–13	0.00021	98,938	20	98,928	6,194,101	62.6
13–14	0.00034	98,918	33	98,901	6,095,173	61.6
14–15	0.00051	98,885	51	98,859	5,996,272	60.6
15–16	0.00070	98,834	69	98,799	5,897,412	59.7
16–17	0.00087	98,765	86	98,722	5,798,613	58.7
17–18	0.00102	98,679	101	98,628	5,699,891	57.8
18–19	0.00113	98,578	112	98,522	5,601,263	56.8
19–20	0.00122	98,466	120	98,406	5,502,741	55.9
20–21	0.00131	98,346	129	98,282	5,404,334	55.0
21–22	0.00141	98,217	138	98,148	5,306,052	54.0
22–23	0.00147	98,079	144	98,007	5,207,904	53.1
23–24	0.00148	97,935	145	97,862	5,109,897	52.2
24–25	0.00145	97,790	142	97,719	5,012,035	51.3
25–26	0.00141	97,648	137	97,580	4,914,316	50.3
26–27	0.00138	97,511	134	97,444	4,816,737	49.4
27–28	0.00136	97,377	133	97,310	4,719,293	48.5
28–29	0.00139	97,244	135	97,176	4,621,983	47.5
29–30	0.00143	97,109	139	97,039	4,524,806	46.6
30–31	0.00149	96,970	144	96,898	4,427,767	45.7
31–32	0.00155	96,826	150	96,751	4,330,869	44.7
32–33	0.00162	96,676	156	96,598	4,234,118	43.8
33–34	0.00170	96,520	164	96,438	4,137,521	42.9
34–35	0.00179	96,356	172	96,270	4,041,083	41.9
35–36	0.00188	96,184	181	96,093	3,944,813	41.0
36–37	0.00199	96,003	191	95,907	3,848,720	40.1
37–38	0.00211	95,812	202	95,711	3,752,813	39.2
38–39	0.00225	95,610	215	95,502	3,657,101	38.3
39–40	0.00243	95,395	232	95,279	3,561,599	37.3
40–41	0.00262	95,163	249	95,039	3,466,320	36.4
41–42	0.00282	94,914	267	94,780	3,371,281	35.5
42–43	0.00304	94,647	287	94,503	3,276,501	34.6
43–44	0.00328	94,359	309	94,205	3,181,998	33.7
44–45	0.00354	94,050	333	93,883	3,087,793	32.8
45–46	0.00385	93,717	360	93,536	2,993,910	31.9
46–47	0.00418	93,356	390	93,161	2,900,374	31.1
47–48	0.00452	92,966	420	92,756	2,807,212	30.2
48–49	0.00486	92,546	450	92,321	2,714,456	29.3
49–50	0.00521	92,096	480	91,856	2,622,136	28.5
50–51	0.00559	91,616	512	91,360	2,530,280	27.6
51–52	0.00601	91,104	548	90,830	2,438,920	26.8
52–53	0.00650	90,556	588	90,262	2,348,090	25.9
53–54	0.00705	89,968	634	89,651	2,257,827	25.1
54–55	0.00769	89,334	687	88,990	2,168,176	24.3
55–56	0.00843	88,646	748	88,273	2,079,186	23.5
56–57	0.00927	87,899	815	87,492	1,990,913	22.7
57–58	0.01019	87,084	888	86,640	1,903,422	21.9
58–59	0.01119	86,197	964	85,715	1,816,782	21.1
59–60	0.01226	85,232	1,045	84,710	1,731,067	20.3
60–61	0.01344	84,188	1,132	83,622	1,646,357	19.6
61–62	0.01477	83,056	1,227	82,442	1,562,735	18.8
62–63	0.01621	81,829	1,327	81,166	1,480,293	18.1
63–64	0.01773	80,502	1,428	79,788	1,399,127	17.4
64–65	0.01932	79,075	1,528	78,311	1,319,339	16.7
65–66	0.02091	77,547	1,621	76,736	1,241,028	16.0
66–67	0.02258	75,926	1,714	75,069	1,164,292	15.3

Table 2. Life table for males: United States, 1998—Con.

Age	Proportion dying during age interval q_x	Number living at beginning of age interval l_x	Number dying during age interval d_x	Stationary population in the age interval L_x	Stationary population in this and all subsequent age intervals T_x	Life expectancy at beginning of age interval e_x
67–68	0.02452	74,211	1,819	73,302	1,089,223	14.7
68–69	0.02683	72,392	1,942	71,421	1,015,921	14.0
69–70	0.02946	70,450	2,076	69,412	944,500	13.4
70–71	0.03225	68,375	2,205	67,272	875,088	12.8
71–72	0.03506	66,170	2,320	65,010	807,816	12.2
72–73	0.03801	63,850	2,427	62,636	742,806	11.6
73–74	0.04108	61,423	2,524	60,161	680,170	11.1
74–75	0.04434	58,899	2,612	57,594	620,008	10.5
75–76	0.04774	56,288	2,687	54,944	562,415	10.0
76–77	0.05138	53,600	2,754	52,223	507,471	9.5
77–78	0.05551	50,847	2,823	49,435	455,247	9.0
78–79	0.06045	48,024	2,903	46,573	405,812	8.5
79–80	0.06635	45,121	2,994	43,624	359,239	8.0
80–81	0.07348	42,127	3,095	40,579	315,615	7.5
81–82	0.08163	39,032	3,186	37,439	275,036	7.0
82–83	0.09038	35,846	3,240	34,226	237,597	6.6
83–84	0.09903	32,606	3,229	30,992	203,371	6.2
84–85	0.10752	29,377	3,159	27,798	172,380	5.9
85–86	0.11761	26,219	3,084	24,677	144,582	5.5
86–87	0.12831	23,135	2,968	21,651	119,905	5.2
87–88	0.13959	20,167	2,815	18,759	98,254	4.9
88–89	0.15146	17,351	2,628	16,037	79,495	4.6
89–90	0.16389	14,723	2,413	13,517	63,458	4.3
90–91	0.17687	12,310	2,177	11,222	49,941	4.1
91–92	0.19035	10,133	1,929	9,169	38,719	3.8
92–93	0.20431	8,204	1,676	7,366	29,551	3.6
93–94	0.21869	6,528	1,428	5,814	22,185	3.4
94–95	0.23346	5,100	1,191	4,505	16,371	3.2
95–96	0.24855	3,910	972	3,424	11,865	3.0
96–97	0.26390	2,938	775	2,550	8,442	2.9
97–98	0.27943	2,163	604	1,860	5,891	2.7
98–99	0.29508	1,558	460	1,328	4,031	2.6
99–100	0.31077	1,098	341	928	2,703	2.5
100+	1.00000	757	757	1,775	1,775	2.3

Table 3. Life table for females: United States, 1998

Age	Proportion dying during age interval q_x	Number living at beginning of age interval l_x	Number dying during age interval d_x	Stationary population in the age interval L_x	Stationary population in this and all subsequent age intervals T_x	Life expectancy at beginning of age interval e_x
0–1	0.00655	100,000	655	99,426	7,947,682	79.5
1–2	0.00051	99,345	51	99,320	7,848,256	79.0
2–3	0.00032	99,294	32	99,278	7,748,936	78.0
3–4	0.00024	99,263	24	99,251	7,649,658	77.1
4–5	0.00019	99,239	19	99,229	7,550,407	76.1
5–6	0.00018	99,220	18	99,211	7,451,178	75.1
6–7	0.00016	99,202	16	99,194	7,351,966	74.1
7–8	0.00015	99,186	15	99,179	7,252,772	73.1
8–9	0.00014	99,171	14	99,164	7,153,593	72.1
9–10	0.00013	99,157	13	99,151	7,054,429	71.1
10–11	0.00013	99,144	12	99,138	6,955,278	70.2
11–12	0.00013	99,132	13	99,125	6,856,141	69.2
12–13	0.00015	99,119	15	99,111	6,757,015	68.2
13–14	0.00020	99,104	20	99,094	6,657,904	67.2
14–15	0.00026	99,084	25	99,072	6,558,810	66.2
15–16	0.00032	99,059	32	99,043	6,459,738	65.2
16–17	0.00039	99,027	38	99,008	6,360,696	64.2
17–18	0.00043	98,988	43	98,967	6,261,688	63.3
18–19	0.00045	98,946	45	98,924	6,162,721	62.3
19–20	0.00045	98,901	45	98,879	6,063,797	61.3
20–21	0.00045	98,857	44	98,835	5,964,918	60.3
21–22	0.00045	98,812	45	98,790	5,866,084	59.4
22–23	0.00046	98,768	45	98,745	5,767,294	58.4
23–24	0.00047	98,722	47	98,699	5,668,549	57.4
24–25	0.00049	98,675	48	98,651	5,569,850	56.4
25–26	0.00051	98,627	50	98,602	5,471,199	55.5
26–27	0.00053	98,577	52	98,551	5,372,597	54.5
27–28	0.00056	98,525	55	98,497	5,274,046	53.5
28–29	0.00059	98,470	58	98,441	5,175,549	52.6
29–30	0.00063	98,412	62	98,381	5,077,107	51.6
30–31	0.00067	98,350	66	98,317	4,978,726	50.6
31–32	0.00072	98,284	71	98,249	4,880,409	49.7
32–33	0.00078	98,213	76	98,175	4,782,160	48.7
33–34	0.00085	98,137	83	98,096	4,683,985	47.7
34–35	0.00092	98,054	90	98,009	4,585,889	46.8
35–36	0.00099	97,964	97	97,915	4,487,880	45.8
36–37	0.00107	97,867	105	97,814	4,389,965	44.9
37–38	0.00115	97,762	113	97,705	4,292,151	43.9
38–39	0.00124	97,649	121	97,589	4,194,445	43.0
39–40	0.00134	97,528	130	97,463	4,096,857	42.0
40–41	0.00144	97,398	140	97,328	3,999,394	41.1
41–42	0.00155	97,257	151	97,182	3,902,066	40.1
42–43	0.00167	97,106	162	97,025	3,804,884	39.2
43–44	0.00180	96,944	174	96,857	3,707,859	38.2
44–45	0.00193	96,770	187	96,676	3,611,003	37.3
45–46	0.00209	96,582	201	96,482	3,514,327	36.4
46–47	0.00226	96,381	218	96,272	3,417,845	35.5
47–48	0.00245	96,163	236	96,046	3,321,573	34.5
48–49	0.00267	95,928	257	95,799	3,225,527	33.6
49–50	0.00292	95,671	279	95,531	3,129,728	32.7
50–51	0.00320	95,392	305	95,239	3,034,197	31.8
51–52	0.00350	95,087	333	94,920	2,938,958	30.9
52–53	0.00383	94,754	363	94,572	2,844,037	30.0
53–54	0.00420	94,390	396	94,192	2,749,466	29.1
54–55	0.00459	93,994	432	93,778	2,655,273	28.2
55–56	0.00506	93,562	473	93,326	2,561,495	27.4
56–57	0.00558	93,089	519	92,830	2,468,169	26.5
57–58	0.00615	92,570	570	92,285	2,375,340	25.7
58–59	0.00676	92,000	622	91,689	2,283,054	24.8
59–60	0.00742	91,378	678	91,039	2,191,365	24.0
60–61	0.00816	90,700	740	90,330	2,100,326	23.2
61–62	0.00900	89,959	810	89,554	2,009,997	22.3
62–63	0.00989	89,150	882	88,709	1,920,442	21.5
63–64	0.01081	88,268	954	87,791	1,831,734	20.8
64–65	0.01175	87,314	1,026	86,801	1,743,943	20.0
65–66	0.01269	86,288	1,095	85,741	1,657,143	19.2
66–67	0.01371	85,193	1,168	84,609	1,571,402	18.4

Table 3. Life table for females: United States, 1998—Con.

Age	Proportion dying during age interval q_x	Number living at beginning of age interval l_x	Number dying during age interval d_x	Stationary population in the age interval L_x	Stationary population in this and all subsequent age intervals T_x	Life expectancy at beginning of age interval e_x
67–68	0.01495	84,025	1,256	83,397	1,486,793	17.7
68–69	0.01645	82,769	1,362	82,088	1,403,396	17.0
69–70	0.01819	81,407	1,481	80,667	1,321,307	16.2
70–71	0.02005	79,926	1,602	79,125	1,240,640	15.5
71–72	0.02195	78,324	1,719	77,464	1,161,515	14.8
72–73	0.02394	76,605	1,834	75,688	1,084,051	14.2
73–74	0.02605	74,771	1,948	73,797	1,008,363	13.5
74–75	0.02832	72,824	2,062	71,793	934,566	12.8
75–76	0.03071	70,761	2,173	69,675	862,773	12.2
76–77	0.03332	68,589	2,286	67,446	793,098	11.6
77–78	0.03642	66,303	2,415	65,096	725,652	10.9
78–79	0.04022	63,888	2,570	62,603	660,556	10.3
79–80	0.04478	61,319	2,746	59,946	597,953	9.8
80–81	0.04996	58,573	2,926	57,109	538,007	9.2
81–82	0.05570	55,646	3,099	54,097	480,898	8.6
82–83	0.06220	52,547	3,268	50,913	426,801	8.1
83–84	0.06949	49,278	3,424	47,566	375,889	7.6
84–85	0.07759	45,854	3,558	44,075	328,322	7.2
85–86	0.08603	42,297	3,639	40,477	284,247	6.7
86–87	0.09510	38,658	3,676	36,820	243,769	6.3
87–88	0.10481	34,982	3,666	33,149	206,950	5.9
88–89	0.11516	31,315	3,606	29,512	173,801	5.6
89–90	0.12615	27,709	3,496	25,961	144,289	5.2
90–91	0.13777	24,214	3,336	22,546	118,328	4.9
91–92	0.15001	20,878	3,132	19,312	95,782	4.6
92–93	0.16284	17,746	2,890	16,301	76,470	4.3
93–94	0.17624	14,856	2,618	13,547	60,170	4.1
94–95	0.19015	12,238	2,327	11,074	46,623	3.8
95–96	0.20455	9,911	2,027	8,897	35,548	3.6
96–97	0.21937	7,883	1,729	7,019	26,651	3.4
97–98	0.23455	6,154	1,443	5,432	19,633	3.2
98–99	0.25003	4,711	1,178	4,122	14,200	3.0
99–100	0.26572	3,533	939	3,063	10,079	2.9
100+	1.00000	2,594	2,594	7,015	7,015	2.7

Table 4. Life table for the white population: United States, 1998

Age	Proportion dying during age interval q_x	Number living at beginning of age interval l_x	Number dying during age interval d_x	Stationary population in the age interval L_x	Stationary population in this and all subsequent age intervals T_x	Life expectancy at beginning of age interval e_x
0–1	0.00596	100,000	596	99,479	7,731,391	77.3
1–2	0.00047	99,404	46	99,380	7,631,912	76.8
2–3	0.00032	99,357	32	99,341	7,532,532	75.8
3–4	0.00023	99,325	23	99,314	7,433,190	74.8
4–5	0.00019	99,303	19	99,293	7,333,876	73.9
5–6	0.00017	99,284	17	99,275	7,234,583	72.9
6–7	0.00017	99,266	17	99,258	7,135,308	71.9
7–8	0.00016	99,250	16	99,242	7,036,050	70.9
8–9	0.00015	99,234	15	99,227	6,936,808	69.9
9–10	0.00013	99,219	13	99,213	6,837,581	68.9
10–11	0.00012	99,206	12	99,200	6,738,368	67.9
11–12	0.00013	99,194	13	99,188	6,639,168	66.9
12–13	0.00017	99,182	17	99,173	6,539,980	65.9
13–14	0.00025	99,165	25	99,152	6,440,807	65.0
14–15	0.00037	99,140	37	99,122	6,341,655	64.0
15–16	0.00050	99,103	49	99,079	6,242,533	63.0
16–17	0.00061	99,054	60	99,024	6,143,454	62.0
17–18	0.00070	98,994	69	98,959	6,044,430	61.1
18–19	0.00075	98,925	74	98,888	5,945,471	60.1
19–20	0.00078	98,850	77	98,812	5,846,583	59.1
20–21	0.00081	98,773	80	98,733	5,747,772	58.2
21–22	0.00085	98,693	84	98,651	5,649,039	57.2
22–23	0.00087	98,609	85	98,566	5,550,388	56.3
23–24	0.00087	98,524	85	98,481	5,451,822	55.3
24–25	0.00085	98,438	84	98,396	5,353,341	54.4
25–26	0.00084	98,354	82	98,313	5,254,944	53.4
26–27	0.00083	98,272	81	98,231	5,156,631	52.5
27–28	0.00083	98,190	82	98,149	5,058,401	51.5
28–29	0.00086	98,108	84	98,066	4,960,251	50.6
29–30	0.00090	98,024	88	97,980	4,862,185	49.6
30–31	0.00094	97,936	92	97,890	4,764,205	48.6
31–32	0.00099	97,844	97	97,795	4,666,314	47.7
32–33	0.00105	97,747	103	97,696	4,568,519	46.7
33–34	0.00112	97,644	110	97,589	4,470,823	45.8
34–35	0.00120	97,535	117	97,476	4,373,234	44.8
35–36	0.00128	97,418	124	97,355	4,275,758	43.9
36–37	0.00136	97,293	132	97,227	4,178,402	42.9
37–38	0.00145	97,161	141	97,090	4,081,175	42.0
38–39	0.00155	97,020	151	96,945	3,984,085	41.1
39–40	0.00167	96,869	162	96,788	3,887,140	40.1
40–41	0.00180	96,707	174	96,620	3,790,352	39.2
41–42	0.00194	96,533	187	96,440	3,693,732	38.3
42–43	0.00209	96,346	201	96,246	3,597,292	37.3
43–44	0.00224	96,145	216	96,037	3,501,047	36.4
44–45	0.00241	95,929	232	95,814	3,405,010	35.5
45–46	0.00261	95,698	249	95,573	3,309,196	34.6
46–47	0.00282	95,448	270	95,314	3,213,623	33.7
47–48	0.00307	95,179	292	95,033	3,118,310	32.8
48–49	0.00333	94,887	316	94,729	3,023,277	31.9
49–50	0.00362	94,571	342	94,400	2,928,548	31.0
50–51	0.00394	94,228	371	94,043	2,834,148	30.1
51–52	0.00430	93,857	403	93,655	2,740,105	29.2
52–53	0.00469	93,454	438	93,235	2,646,450	28.3
53–54	0.00512	93,016	476	92,778	2,553,215	27.4
54–55	0.00561	92,540	519	92,280	2,460,438	26.6
55–56	0.00618	92,021	568	91,737	2,368,157	25.7
56–57	0.00682	91,453	624	91,141	2,276,421	24.9
57–58	0.00754	90,829	684	90,486	2,185,280	24.1
58–59	0.00829	90,144	748	89,770	2,094,794	23.2
59–60	0.00911	89,396	814	88,989	2,005,024	22.4
60–61	0.01002	88,582	888	88,138	1,916,034	21.6
61–62	0.01106	87,694	970	87,210	1,827,896	20.8
62–63	0.01219	86,725	1,057	86,196	1,740,687	20.1
63–64	0.01340	85,668	1,148	85,094	1,654,490	19.3
64–65	0.01467	84,520	1,240	83,900	1,569,396	18.6
65–66	0.01594	83,280	1,328	82,617	1,485,496	17.8
66–67	0.01730	81,953	1,418	81,244	1,402,880	17.1

Table 4. Life table for the white population: United States, 1998—Con.

Age	Proportion dying during age interval q_x	Number living at beginning of age interval l_x	Number dying during age interval d_x	Stationary population in the age interval L_x	Stationary population in this and all subsequent age intervals T_x	Life expectancy at beginning of age interval e_x
67–68	0.01887	80,534	1,519	79,775	1,321,636	16.4
68–69	0.02070	79,015	1,636	78,197	1,241,861	15.7
69–70	0.02276	77,379	1,761	76,499	1,163,664	15.0
70–71	0.02491	75,618	1,884	74,676	1,087,165	14.4
71–72	0.02710	73,734	1,998	72,735	1,012,489	13.7
72–73	0.02940	71,736	2,109	70,682	939,754	13.1
73–74	0.03187	69,627	2,219	68,518	869,072	12.5
74–75	0.03456	67,408	2,329	66,243	800,554	11.9
75–76	0.03737	65,079	2,432	63,863	734,311	11.3
76–77	0.04040	62,647	2,531	61,381	670,448	10.7
77–78	0.04390	60,116	2,639	58,796	609,067	10.1
78–79	0.04810	57,477	2,765	56,095	550,271	9.6
79–80	0.05310	54,712	2,905	53,260	494,176	9.0
80–81	0.05888	51,807	3,051	50,282	440,916	8.5
81–82	0.06534	48,757	3,186	47,164	390,634	8.0
82–83	0.07244	45,571	3,301	43,920	343,471	7.5
83–84	0.08000	42,270	3,382	40,579	299,550	7.1
84–85	0.08807	38,888	3,425	37,176	258,972	6.7
85–86	0.09673	35,463	3,430	33,748	221,796	6.3
86–87	0.10603	32,033	3,396	30,335	188,048	5.9
87–88	0.11601	28,636	3,322	26,975	157,714	5.5
88–89	0.12669	25,314	3,207	23,711	130,738	5.2
89–90	0.13808	22,107	3,053	20,581	107,027	4.8
90–91	0.15022	19,055	2,862	17,624	86,446	4.5
91–92	0.16311	16,192	2,641	14,872	68,823	4.3
92–93	0.17677	13,551	2,396	12,353	53,951	4.0
93–94	0.19122	11,156	2,133	10,089	41,597	3.7
94–95	0.20645	9,023	1,863	8,091	31,508	3.5
95–96	0.22247	7,160	1,593	6,363	23,417	3.3
96–97	0.23928	5,567	1,332	4,901	17,054	3.1
97–98	0.25687	4,235	1,088	3,691	12,153	2.9
98–99	0.27524	3,147	866	2,714	8,462	2.7
99–100	0.29435	2,281	671	1,945	5,748	2.5
100+	1.00000	1,609	1,609	3,803	3,803	2.4

Table 5. Life table for white males: United States, 1998

Age	Proportion dying during age interval q_x	Number living at beginning of age interval l_x	Number dying during age interval d_x	Stationary population in the age interval L_x	Stationary population in this and all subsequent age intervals T_x	Life expectancy at beginning of age interval e_x
0–1.	0.00648	100,000	648	99,435	7,452,750	74.5
1–2.	0.00049	99,352	49	99,328	7,353,314	74.0
2–3.	0.00036	99,303	35	99,286	7,253,987	73.0
3–4.	0.00025	99,268	25	99,255	7,154,701	72.1
4–5.	0.00021	99,243	21	99,233	7,055,446	71.1
5–6.	0.00020	99,222	19	99,213	6,956,213	70.1
6–7.	0.00019	99,203	19	99,193	6,857,001	69.1
7–8.	0.00018	99,184	18	99,175	6,757,807	68.1
8–9.	0.00017	99,166	17	99,157	6,658,632	67.1
9–10.	0.00015	99,149	15	99,142	6,559,475	66.2
10–11.	0.00013	99,134	13	99,128	6,460,333	65.2
11–12.	0.00013	99,122	13	99,115	6,361,205	64.2
12–13.	0.00019	99,109	19	99,099	6,262,090	63.2
13–14.	0.00031	99,090	31	99,074	6,162,991	62.2
14–15.	0.00047	99,059	47	99,036	6,063,916	61.2
15–16.	0.00065	99,012	64	98,980	5,964,881	60.2
16–17.	0.00081	98,948	80	98,908	5,865,901	59.3
17–18.	0.00094	98,868	93	98,821	5,766,993	58.3
18–19.	0.00104	98,775	102	98,724	5,668,171	57.4
19–20.	0.00111	98,673	109	98,618	5,569,448	56.4
20–21.	0.00118	98,563	116	98,505	5,470,830	55.5
21–22.	0.00126	98,447	124	98,385	5,372,325	54.6
22–23.	0.00130	98,323	128	98,259	5,273,940	53.6
23–24.	0.00130	98,195	128	98,131	5,175,681	52.7
24–25.	0.00127	98,066	125	98,004	5,077,551	51.8
25–26.	0.00123	97,942	120	97,882	4,979,547	50.8
26–27.	0.00120	97,821	117	97,763	4,881,665	49.9
27–28.	0.00119	97,704	116	97,646	4,783,902	49.0
28–29.	0.00121	97,588	118	97,530	4,686,256	48.0
29–30.	0.00125	97,471	122	97,409	4,588,726	47.1
30–31.	0.00131	97,348	128	97,285	4,491,317	46.1
31–32.	0.00137	97,221	133	97,154	4,394,032	45.2
32–33.	0.00144	97,088	140	97,018	4,296,878	44.3
33–34.	0.00152	96,948	147	96,875	4,199,860	43.3
34–35.	0.00160	96,801	155	96,724	4,102,985	42.4
35–36.	0.00169	96,646	164	96,564	4,006,261	41.5
36–37.	0.00179	96,483	173	96,396	3,909,697	40.5
37–38.	0.00190	96,310	183	96,218	3,813,301	39.6
38–39.	0.00203	96,127	195	96,029	3,717,082	38.7
39–40.	0.00219	95,931	210	95,827	3,621,053	37.7
40–41.	0.00236	95,722	226	95,609	3,525,227	36.8
41–42.	0.00254	95,496	242	95,375	3,429,618	35.9
42–43.	0.00273	95,254	260	95,124	3,334,243	35.0
43–44.	0.00294	94,993	279	94,854	3,239,119	34.1
44–45.	0.00317	94,714	300	94,564	3,144,266	33.2
45–46.	0.00342	94,414	323	94,253	3,049,701	32.3
46–47.	0.00371	94,091	349	93,917	2,955,448	31.4
47–48.	0.00401	93,743	376	93,554	2,861,531	30.5
48–49.	0.00433	93,366	404	93,164	2,767,977	29.6
49–50.	0.00466	92,962	434	92,745	2,674,813	28.8
50–51.	0.00503	92,528	465	92,296	2,582,068	27.9
51–52.	0.00544	92,063	501	91,813	2,489,772	27.0
52–53.	0.00590	91,562	540	91,292	2,397,960	26.2
53–54.	0.00643	91,022	585	90,729	2,306,668	25.3
54–55.	0.00704	90,437	637	90,118	2,215,938	24.5
55–56.	0.00776	89,800	697	89,451	2,125,820	23.7
56–57.	0.00858	89,103	764	88,721	2,036,369	22.9
57–58.	0.00947	88,339	837	87,920	1,947,648	22.0
58–59.	0.01042	87,502	912	87,046	1,859,728	21.3
59–60.	0.01144	86,590	990	86,095	1,772,682	20.5
60–61.	0.01256	85,600	1,075	85,063	1,686,586	19.7
61–62.	0.01384	84,525	1,170	83,940	1,601,524	18.9
62–63.	0.01526	83,356	1,272	82,719	1,517,583	18.2
63–64.	0.01682	82,083	1,381	81,393	1,434,864	17.5
64–65.	0.01848	80,703	1,492	79,957	1,353,471	16.8
65–66.	0.02016	79,211	1,597	78,412	1,273,514	16.1
66–67.	0.02193	77,614	1,702	76,763	1,195,101	15.4

Table 5. Life table for white males: United States, 1998—Con.

Age	Proportion dying during age interval q_x	Number living at beginning of age interval l_x	Number dying during age interval d_x	Stationary population in the age interval L_x	Stationary population in this and all subsequent age intervals T_x	Life expectancy at beginning of age interval e_x
67–68	0.02394	75,912	1,817	75,003	1,118,339	14.7
68–69	0.02627	74,095	1,946	73,121	1,043,336	14.1
69–70	0.02887	72,148	2,083	71,107	970,214	13.4
70–71	0.03160	70,065	2,214	68,958	899,107	12.8
71–72	0.03435	67,851	2,331	66,686	830,149	12.2
72–73	0.03724	65,521	2,440	64,301	763,463	11.7
73–74	0.04031	63,081	2,543	61,810	699,162	11.1
74–75	0.04360	60,538	2,640	59,218	637,352	10.5
75–76	0.04705	57,899	2,724	56,537	578,134	10.0
76–77	0.05072	55,175	2,799	53,775	521,597	9.5
77–78	0.05493	52,376	2,877	50,938	467,822	8.9
78–79	0.05996	49,499	2,968	48,015	416,884	8.4
79–80	0.06597	46,531	3,070	44,996	368,869	7.9
80–81	0.07321	43,462	3,182	41,871	323,873	7.5
81–82	0.08147	40,280	3,282	38,639	282,002	7.0
82–83	0.09031	36,998	3,341	35,328	243,363	6.6
83–84	0.09905	33,657	3,334	31,990	208,036	6.2
84–85	0.10768	30,323	3,265	28,691	176,045	5.8
85–86	0.11798	27,058	3,192	25,462	147,355	5.4
86–87	0.12896	23,866	3,078	22,327	121,892	5.1
87–88	0.14062	20,788	2,923	19,327	99,565	4.8
88–89	0.15297	17,865	2,733	16,499	80,239	4.5
89–90	0.16601	15,132	2,512	13,876	63,740	4.2
90–91	0.17973	12,620	2,268	11,486	49,864	4.0
91–92	0.19412	10,352	2,010	9,347	38,377	3.7
92–93	0.20916	8,343	1,745	7,470	29,030	3.5
93–94	0.22483	6,598	1,483	5,856	21,560	3.3
94–95	0.24109	5,114	1,233	4,498	15,704	3.1
95–96	0.25792	3,881	1,001	3,381	11,206	2.9
96–97	0.27526	2,880	793	2,484	7,826	2.7
97–98	0.29307	2,087	612	1,782	5,342	2.6
98–99	0.31128	1,476	459	1,246	3,560	2.4
99–100	0.32983	1,016	335	849	2,314	2.3
100+	1.00000	681	681	1,466	1,466	2.2

Table 6. Life table for white females: United States, 1998

Age	Proportion dying during age interval q_x	Number living at beginning of age interval l_x	Number dying during age interval d_x	Stationary population in the age interval L_x	Stationary population in this and all subsequent age intervals T_x	Life expectancy at beginning of age interval e_x
0–1	0.00542	100,000	542	99,524	7,999,603	80.0
1–2	0.00044	99,458	44	99,436	7,900,079	79.4
2–3	0.00028	99,414	28	99,400	7,800,643	78.5
3–4	0.00021	99,386	21	99,376	7,701,243	77.5
4–5	0.00017	99,365	17	99,357	7,601,867	76.5
5–6	0.00015	99,348	15	99,341	7,502,511	75.5
6–7	0.00014	99,333	14	99,326	7,403,170	74.5
7–8	0.00013	99,319	13	99,312	7,303,844	73.5
8–9	0.00013	99,306	13	99,299	7,204,532	72.5
9–10	0.00012	99,293	12	99,287	7,105,232	71.6
10–11	0.00011	99,281	11	99,276	7,005,945	70.6
11–12	0.00012	99,270	12	99,264	6,906,669	69.6
12–13	0.00014	99,258	14	99,251	6,807,405	68.6
13–14	0.00019	99,244	19	99,234	6,708,154	67.6
14–15	0.00026	99,225	26	99,212	6,608,920	66.6
15–16	0.00033	99,199	33	99,183	6,509,708	65.6
16–17	0.00040	99,166	39	99,147	6,410,525	64.6
17–18	0.00044	99,127	43	99,105	6,311,379	63.7
18–19	0.00045	99,083	45	99,061	6,212,274	62.7
19–20	0.00044	99,039	43	99,017	6,113,212	61.7
20–21	0.00042	98,995	42	98,975	6,014,195	60.8
21–22	0.00041	98,954	41	98,934	5,915,221	59.8
22–23	0.00040	98,913	40	98,893	5,816,287	58.8
23–24	0.00041	98,873	40	98,853	5,717,394	57.8
24–25	0.00042	98,833	42	98,812	5,618,540	56.8
25–26	0.00044	98,791	43	98,770	5,519,728	55.9
26–27	0.00046	98,748	45	98,725	5,420,959	54.9
27–28	0.00048	98,703	47	98,679	5,322,233	53.9
28–29	0.00051	98,656	50	98,631	5,223,554	52.9
29–30	0.00054	98,606	53	98,579	5,124,924	52.0
30–31	0.00057	98,553	57	98,524	5,026,344	51.0
31–32	0.00061	98,496	61	98,466	4,927,820	50.0
32–33	0.00066	98,436	65	98,403	4,829,354	49.1
33–34	0.00072	98,370	71	98,335	4,730,951	48.1
34–35	0.00079	98,299	78	98,260	4,632,616	47.1
35–36	0.00086	98,221	84	98,179	4,534,356	46.2
36–37	0.00093	98,137	91	98,092	4,436,177	45.2
37–38	0.00100	98,046	98	97,997	4,338,085	44.2
38–39	0.00107	97,949	105	97,896	4,240,088	43.3
39–40	0.00115	97,844	113	97,788	4,142,192	42.3
40–41	0.00124	97,731	121	97,671	4,044,404	41.4
41–42	0.00134	97,610	130	97,545	3,946,734	40.4
42–43	0.00144	97,480	140	97,410	3,849,189	39.5
43–44	0.00155	97,339	151	97,264	3,751,779	38.5
44–45	0.00167	97,189	162	97,108	3,654,515	37.6
45–46	0.00180	97,027	174	96,940	3,557,407	36.7
46–47	0.00195	96,853	189	96,758	3,460,467	35.7
47–48	0.00213	96,664	206	96,561	3,363,709	34.8
48–49	0.00235	96,458	227	96,345	3,267,148	33.9
49–50	0.00260	96,231	250	96,106	3,170,803	32.9
50–51	0.00288	95,981	277	95,843	3,074,697	32.0
51–52	0.00319	95,705	305	95,552	2,978,854	31.1
52–53	0.00351	95,400	335	95,232	2,883,302	30.2
53–54	0.00385	95,065	366	94,882	2,788,070	29.3
54–55	0.00423	94,698	400	94,498	2,693,188	28.4
55–56	0.00466	94,298	440	94,078	2,598,690	27.6
56–57	0.00516	93,858	485	93,616	2,504,612	26.7
57–58	0.00571	93,374	533	93,107	2,410,995	25.8
58–59	0.00630	92,841	585	92,548	2,317,888	25.0
59–60	0.00693	92,256	640	91,936	2,225,340	24.1
60–61	0.00765	91,616	701	91,266	2,133,404	23.3
61–62	0.00848	90,915	771	90,530	2,042,138	22.5
62–63	0.00936	90,144	844	89,722	1,951,608	21.6
63–64	0.01028	89,300	918	88,841	1,861,886	20.8
64–65	0.01123	88,382	993	87,886	1,773,044	20.1
65–66	0.01219	87,390	1,066	86,857	1,685,158	19.3
66–67	0.01324	86,324	1,143	85,753	1,598,301	18.5

Table 6. Life table for white females: United States, 1998—Con.

Age	Proportion dying during age interval	Number living at beginning of age interval	Number dying during age interval	Stationary population in the age interval	Stationary population in this and all subsequent age intervals	Life expectancy at beginning of age interval
	q_x	l_x	d_x	L_x	T_x	e_x
67–68	0.01448	85,181	1,233	84,564	1,512,549	17.8
68–69	0.01596	83,948	1,340	83,278	1,427,984	17.0
69–70	0.01764	82,608	1,457	81,879	1,344,706	16.3
70–71	0.01941	81,151	1,575	80,363	1,262,827	15.6
71–72	0.02123	79,575	1,689	78,731	1,182,464	14.9
72–73	0.02317	77,886	1,805	76,984	1,103,733	14.2
73–74	0.02528	76,082	1,924	75,120	1,026,749	13.5
74–75	0.02761	74,158	2,047	73,134	951,630	12.8
75–76	0.03007	72,110	2,169	71,026	878,495	12.2
76–77	0.03275	69,942	2,291	68,796	807,469	11.5
77–78	0.03591	67,651	2,430	66,436	738,673	10.9
78–79	0.03976	65,221	2,593	63,925	672,237	10.3
79–80	0.04433	62,628	2,776	61,240	608,312	9.7
80–81	0.04950	59,852	2,963	58,371	547,071	9.1
81–82	0.05523	56,889	3,142	55,318	488,701	8.6
82–83	0.06174	53,747	3,318	52,088	433,382	8.1
83–84	0.06908	50,429	3,484	48,687	381,294	7.6
84–85	0.07731	46,945	3,630	45,131	332,607	7.1
85–86	0.08581	43,316	3,717	41,457	287,476	6.6
86–87	0.09501	39,599	3,762	37,718	246,019	6.2
87–88	0.10494	35,836	3,761	33,956	208,301	5.8
88–89	0.11563	32,076	3,709	30,221	174,345	5.4
89–90	0.12710	28,367	3,605	26,564	144,124	5.1
90–91	0.13937	24,761	3,451	23,036	117,560	4.7
91–92	0.15245	21,310	3,249	19,686	94,524	4.4
92–93	0.16635	18,062	3,005	16,559	74,838	4.1
93–94	0.18108	15,057	2,726	13,694	58,279	3.9
94–95	0.19663	12,331	2,425	11,118	44,585	3.6
95–96	0.21300	9,906	2,110	8,851	33,467	3.4
96–97	0.23018	7,796	1,794	6,899	24,616	3.2
97–98	0.24814	6,002	1,489	5,257	17,717	3.0
98–99	0.26685	4,512	1,204	3,910	12,460	2.8
99–100	0.28627	3,308	947	2,835	8,550	2.6
100+	1.00000	2,361	2,361	5,715	5,715	2.4

Table 7. Life table for the black population: United States, 1998

Age	Proportion dying during age interval q_x	Number living at beginning of age interval l_x	Number dying during age interval d_x	Stationary population in the age interval L_x	Stationary population in this and all subsequent age intervals T_x	Life expectancy at beginning of age interval e_x
0–1	0.01434	100,000	1,434	98,744	7,134,434	71.3
1–2	0.00103	98,566	102	98,515	7,035,690	71.4
2–3	0.00060	98,464	59	98,435	6,937,175	70.5
3–4	0.00048	98,405	47	98,382	6,838,740	69.5
4–5	0.00036	98,358	35	98,340	6,740,359	68.5
5–6	0.00035	98,323	34	98,306	6,642,018	67.6
6–7	0.00032	98,289	31	98,273	6,543,712	66.6
7–8	0.00029	98,257	29	98,243	6,445,439	65.6
8–9	0.00026	98,228	26	98,216	6,347,197	64.6
9–10	0.00023	98,203	22	98,191	6,248,981	63.6
10–11	0.00020	98,180	19	98,170	6,150,790	62.6
11–12	0.00019	98,161	19	98,151	6,052,619	61.7
12–13	0.00024	98,142	24	98,130	5,954,468	60.7
13–14	0.00035	98,118	35	98,101	5,856,338	59.7
14–15	0.00051	98,083	50	98,058	5,758,238	58.7
15–16	0.00068	98,033	67	98,000	5,660,179	57.7
16–17	0.00084	97,967	82	97,925	5,562,179	56.8
17–18	0.00099	97,884	97	97,836	5,464,254	55.8
18–19	0.00112	97,788	110	97,733	5,366,418	54.9
19–20	0.00125	97,678	122	97,617	5,268,685	53.9
20–21	0.00139	97,556	135	97,488	5,171,068	53.0
21–22	0.00154	97,421	150	97,346	5,073,580	52.1
22–23	0.00165	97,271	161	97,191	4,976,234	51.2
23–24	0.00172	97,110	167	97,027	4,879,044	50.2
24–25	0.00173	96,943	168	96,859	4,782,017	49.3
25–26	0.00174	96,775	168	96,691	4,685,157	48.4
26–27	0.00176	96,607	170	96,522	4,588,466	47.5
27–28	0.00179	96,438	172	96,351	4,491,943	46.6
28–29	0.00184	96,265	177	96,177	4,395,592	45.7
29–30	0.00191	96,088	184	95,996	4,299,416	44.7
30–31	0.00199	95,904	191	95,808	4,203,420	43.8
31–32	0.00208	95,713	199	95,613	4,107,611	42.9
32–33	0.00219	95,513	209	95,409	4,011,998	42.0
33–34	0.00233	95,304	222	95,193	3,916,589	41.1
34–35	0.00248	95,082	236	94,964	3,821,396	40.2
35–36	0.00265	94,846	251	94,720	3,726,432	39.3
36–37	0.00282	94,595	267	94,461	3,631,712	38.4
37–38	0.00302	94,328	285	94,185	3,537,250	37.5
38–39	0.00327	94,043	307	93,889	3,443,065	36.6
39–40	0.00355	93,736	332	93,569	3,349,176	35.7
40–41	0.00385	93,403	359	93,223	3,255,606	34.9
41–42	0.00416	93,044	387	92,850	3,162,383	34.0
42–43	0.00451	92,657	418	92,448	3,069,533	33.1
43–44	0.00491	92,238	453	92,012	2,977,085	32.3
44–45	0.00536	91,785	492	91,539	2,885,073	31.4
45–46	0.00588	91,293	536	91,025	2,793,534	30.6
46–47	0.00643	90,757	583	90,465	2,702,510	29.8
47–48	0.00696	90,173	628	89,859	2,612,045	29.0
48–49	0.00745	89,545	667	89,212	2,522,186	28.2
49–50	0.00792	88,878	704	88,526	2,432,974	27.4
50–51	0.00842	88,174	742	87,803	2,344,448	26.6
51–52	0.00902	87,432	788	87,038	2,256,645	25.8
52–53	0.00968	86,643	839	86,224	2,169,607	25.0
53–54	0.01042	85,804	894	85,357	2,083,383	24.3
54–55	0.01122	84,910	952	84,434	1,998,026	23.5
55–56	0.01205	83,958	1,011	83,452	1,913,592	22.8
56–57	0.01294	82,947	1,073	82,410	1,830,139	22.1
57–58	0.01394	81,874	1,142	81,303	1,747,729	21.3
58–59	0.01510	80,732	1,219	80,122	1,666,426	20.6
59–60	0.01639	79,513	1,303	78,861	1,586,304	20.0
60–61	0.01783	78,210	1,394	77,513	1,507,442	19.3
61–62	0.01932	76,815	1,484	76,073	1,429,930	18.6
62–63	0.02070	75,332	1,559	74,552	1,353,856	18.0
63–64	0.02184	73,772	1,611	72,967	1,279,304	17.3
64–65	0.02280	72,162	1,645	71,339	1,206,337	16.7
65–66	0.02359	70,516	1,664	69,685	1,134,998	16.1
66–67	0.02451	68,853	1,688	68,009	1,065,314	15.5

Table 7. Life table for the black population: United States, 1998—Con.

Age	Proportion dying during age interval q_x	Number living at beginning of age interval l_x	Number dying during age interval d_x	Stationary population in the age interval L_x	Stationary population in this and all subsequent age intervals T_x	Life expectancy at beginning of age interval e_x
67–68	0.02593	67,165	1,741	66,294	997,305	14.8
68–69	0.02815	65,424	1,841	64,503	931,010	14.2
69–70	0.03111	63,582	1,978	62,593	866,507	13.6
70–71	0.03460	61,604	2,132	60,538	803,914	13.0
71–72	0.03819	59,472	2,272	58,337	743,376	12.5
72–73	0.04165	57,201	2,383	56,010	685,039	12.0
73–74	0.04456	54,818	2,443	53,597	629,029	11.5
74–75	0.04698	52,375	2,461	51,145	575,433	11.0
75–76	0.04928	49,915	2,460	48,685	524,287	10.5
76–77	0.05190	47,455	2,463	46,224	475,602	10.0
77–78	0.05496	44,992	2,473	43,756	429,379	9.5
78–79	0.05888	42,520	2,503	41,268	385,622	9.1
79–80	0.06382	40,016	2,554	38,740	344,354	8.6
80–81	0.06974	37,463	2,613	36,156	305,615	8.2
81–82	0.07637	34,850	2,662	33,519	269,458	7.7
82–83	0.08364	32,189	2,692	30,842	235,939	7.3
83–84	0.09092	29,496	2,682	28,156	205,097	7.0
84–85	0.09794	26,815	2,626	25,502	176,941	6.6
85–86	0.10523	24,189	2,545	22,916	151,440	6.3
86–87	0.11295	21,643	2,445	20,421	128,524	5.9
87–88	0.12111	19,198	2,325	18,036	108,103	5.6
88–89	0.12972	16,873	2,189	15,779	90,067	5.3
89–90	0.13879	14,685	2,038	13,666	74,288	5.1
90–91	0.14833	12,647	1,876	11,709	60,623	4.8
91–92	0.15836	10,771	1,706	9,918	48,914	4.5
92–93	0.16889	9,065	1,531	8,299	38,996	4.3
93–94	0.17993	7,534	1,356	6,856	30,697	4.1
94–95	0.19148	6,178	1,183	5,587	23,841	3.9
95–96	0.20356	4,995	1,017	4,487	18,254	3.7
96–97	0.21617	3,978	860	3,548	13,767	3.5
97–98	0.22931	3,118	715	2,761	10,218	3.3
98–99	0.24300	2,403	584	2,111	7,458	3.1
99–100	0.25722	1,819	468	1,585	5,346	2.9
100+	1.00000	1,351	1,351	3,761	3,761	2.8

Table 8. Life table for black males: United States, 1998

Age	Proportion dying during age interval q_x	Number living at beginning of age interval l_x	Number dying during age interval d_x	Stationary population in the age interval L_x	Stationary population in this and all subsequent age intervals T_x	Life expectancy at beginning of age interval e_x
0–1	0.01579	100,000	1,579	98,614	6,761,111	67.6
1–2	0.00116	98,421	114	98,364	6,662,497	67.7
2–3	0.00067	98,307	66	98,274	6,564,133	66.8
3–4	0.00052	98,241	51	98,215	6,465,859	65.8
4–5	0.00042	98,190	42	98,169	6,367,644	64.9
5–6	0.00039	98,149	38	98,130	6,269,475	63.9
6–7	0.00037	98,111	36	98,093	6,171,345	62.9
7–8	0.00034	98,075	34	98,058	6,073,252	61.9
8–9	0.00030	98,041	30	98,026	5,975,195	60.9
9–10	0.00025	98,011	25	97,999	5,877,168	60.0
10–11	0.00021	97,986	20	97,976	5,779,169	59.0
11–12	0.00020	97,966	20	97,956	5,681,193	58.0
12–13	0.00029	97,946	28	97,932	5,583,237	57.0
13–14	0.00048	97,918	47	97,895	5,485,305	56.0
14–15	0.00074	97,871	72	97,835	5,387,411	55.0
15–16	0.00102	97,799	100	97,749	5,289,576	54.1
16–17	0.00128	97,699	125	97,636	5,191,827	53.1
17–18	0.00152	97,573	149	97,499	5,094,191	52.2
18–19	0.00174	97,425	169	97,340	4,996,692	51.3
19–20	0.00193	97,256	188	97,162	4,899,352	50.4
20–21	0.00216	97,068	210	96,963	4,802,190	49.5
21–22	0.00240	96,858	232	96,742	4,705,227	48.6
22–23	0.00257	96,626	249	96,501	4,608,486	47.7
23–24	0.00265	96,377	256	96,249	4,511,984	46.8
24–25	0.00265	96,121	255	95,994	4,415,735	45.9
25–26	0.00262	95,867	251	95,741	4,319,741	45.1
26–27	0.00261	95,615	249	95,491	4,224,000	44.2
27–28	0.00261	95,366	249	95,242	4,128,509	43.3
28–29	0.00264	95,117	251	94,992	4,033,267	42.4
29–30	0.00271	94,866	257	94,737	3,938,276	41.5
30–31	0.00278	94,609	263	94,478	3,843,538	40.6
31–32	0.00286	94,346	270	94,211	3,749,061	39.7
32–33	0.00296	94,077	279	93,937	3,654,849	38.8
33–34	0.00310	93,798	290	93,653	3,560,912	38.0
34–35	0.00326	93,508	305	93,355	3,467,259	37.1
35–36	0.00343	93,203	319	93,043	3,373,904	36.2
36–37	0.00362	92,884	336	92,716	3,280,860	35.3
37–38	0.00385	92,548	356	92,370	3,188,144	34.4
38–39	0.00415	92,192	382	92,000	3,095,775	33.6
39–40	0.00450	91,809	413	91,602	3,003,774	32.7
40–41	0.00488	91,396	446	91,173	2,912,172	31.9
41–42	0.00529	90,949	481	90,709	2,820,999	31.0
42–43	0.00576	90,468	521	90,208	2,730,290	30.2
43–44	0.00632	89,948	568	89,663	2,640,082	29.4
44–45	0.00696	89,379	622	89,068	2,550,419	28.5
45–46	0.00771	88,757	685	88,415	2,461,351	27.7
46–47	0.00852	88,073	751	87,697	2,372,936	26.9
47–48	0.00931	87,322	813	86,915	2,285,239	26.2
48–49	0.01001	86,509	866	86,076	2,198,323	25.4
49–50	0.01065	85,643	912	85,187	2,112,247	24.7
50–51	0.01134	84,731	961	84,251	2,027,060	23.9
51–52	0.01216	83,770	1,019	83,261	1,942,809	23.2
52–53	0.01306	82,751	1,080	82,211	1,859,549	22.5
53–54	0.01402	81,671	1,145	81,098	1,777,338	21.8
54–55	0.01504	80,526	1,211	79,920	1,696,239	21.1
55–56	0.01608	79,315	1,275	78,677	1,616,319	20.4
56–57	0.01719	78,040	1,342	77,369	1,537,641	19.7
57–58	0.01849	76,698	1,418	75,989	1,460,272	19.0
58–59	0.02006	75,280	1,510	74,525	1,384,283	18.4
59–60	0.02185	73,770	1,612	72,964	1,309,759	17.8
60–61	0.02387	72,158	1,722	71,297	1,236,795	17.1
61–62	0.02592	70,436	1,825	69,523	1,165,497	16.5
62–63	0.02772	68,610	1,902	67,659	1,095,974	16.0
63–64	0.02904	66,709	1,937	65,740	1,028,315	15.4
64–65	0.02998	64,771	1,942	63,800	962,575	14.9
65–66	0.03064	62,829	1,925	61,867	898,775	14.3
66–67	0.03146	60,904	1,916	59,946	836,908	13.7

Table 8. Life table for black males: United States, 1998—Con.

Age	Proportion dying during age interval	Number living at beginning of age interval	Number dying during age interval	Stationary population in the age interval	Stationary population in this and all subsequent age intervals	Life expectancy at beginning of age interval
	q_x	l_x	d_x	L_x	T_x	e_x
67–68.	0.03291	58,988	1,941	58,017	776,962	13.2
68–69.	0.03540	57,047	2,020	56,037	718,945	12.6
69–70.	0.03890	55,027	2,141	53,957	662,908	12.0
70–71.	0.04307	52,886	2,278	51,747	608,951	11.5
71–72.	0.04738	50,608	2,398	49,409	557,204	11.0
72–73.	0.05165	48,210	2,490	46,966	507,795	10.5
73–74.	0.05533	45,721	2,530	44,456	460,829	10.1
74–75.	0.05843	43,191	2,524	41,929	416,373	9.6
75–76.	0.06144	40,667	2,499	39,418	374,444	9.2
76–77.	0.06483	38,169	2,475	36,931	335,026	8.8
77–78.	0.06861	35,694	2,449	34,470	298,094	8.4
78–79.	0.07324	33,245	2,435	32,028	263,625	7.9
79–80.	0.07904	30,810	2,435	29,593	231,597	7.5
80–81.	0.08629	28,375	2,448	27,151	202,004	7.1
81–82.	0.09477	25,927	2,457	24,698	174,853	6.7
82–83.	0.10399	23,470	2,441	22,249	150,155	6.4
83–84.	0.11248	21,029	2,365	19,846	127,906	6.1
84–85.	0.11945	18,664	2,229	17,549	108,059	5.8
85–86.	0.12760	16,434	2,097	15,386	90,510	5.5
86–87.	0.13610	14,337	1,951	13,362	75,125	5.2
87–88.	0.14493	12,386	1,795	11,488	61,763	5.0
88–89.	0.15409	10,591	1,632	9,775	50,275	4.7
89–90.	0.16357	8,959	1,465	8,226	40,500	4.5
90–91.	0.17335	7,494	1,299	6,844	32,274	4.3
91–92.	0.18343	6,195	1,136	5,626	25,430	4.1
92–93.	0.19378	5,058	980	4,568	19,803	3.9
93–94.	0.20440	4,078	834	3,661	15,235	3.7
94–95.	0.21525	3,245	698	2,895	11,574	3.6
95–96.	0.22632	2,546	576	2,258	8,678	3.4
96–97.	0.23758	1,970	468	1,736	6,420	3.3
97–98.	0.24901	1,502	374	1,315	4,685	3.1
98–99.	0.26057	1,128	294	981	3,370	3.0
99–100	0.27223	834	227	720	2,389	2.9
100+.	1.00000	607	607	1,668	1,668	2.7

Table 9. Life table for black females: United States, 1998

Age	Proportion dying during age interval	Number living at beginning of age interval	Number dying during age interval	Stationary population in the age interval	Stationary population in this and all subsequent age intervals	Life expectancy at beginning of age interval
	q_x	l_x	d_x	L_x	T_x	e_x
0–1.	0.01285	100,000	1,285	98,877	7,479,822	74.8
1–2.	0.00090	98,715	89	98,671	7,380,945	74.8
2–3.	0.00052	98,626	51	98,601	7,282,274	73.8
3–4.	0.00044	98,575	44	98,554	7,183,673	72.9
4–5.	0.00029	98,532	29	98,517	7,085,120	71.9
5–6.	0.00031	98,503	30	98,488	6,986,602	70.9
6–7.	0.00027	98,473	27	98,459	6,888,115	69.9
7–8.	0.00024	98,446	24	98,434	6,789,655	69.0
8–9.	0.00022	98,422	22	98,411	6,691,221	68.0
9–10.	0.00020	98,400	20	98,390	6,592,810	67.0
10–11.	0.00019	98,380	18	98,371	6,494,420	66.0
11–12.	0.00018	98,362	18	98,353	6,396,049	65.0
12–13.	0.00019	98,344	19	98,334	6,297,696	64.0
13–14.	0.00023	98,325	22	98,314	6,199,362	63.0
14–15.	0.00027	98,303	27	98,289	6,101,048	62.1
15–16.	0.00032	98,276	32	98,260	6,002,759	61.1
16–17.	0.00038	98,244	37	98,225	5,904,499	60.1
17–18.	0.00043	98,207	43	98,185	5,806,274	59.1
18–19.	0.00049	98,164	48	98,140	5,708,088	58.1
19–20.	0.00054	98,116	53	98,090	5,609,948	57.2
20–21.	0.00061	98,063	60	98,033	5,511,858	56.2
21–22.	0.00069	98,003	67	97,969	5,413,825	55.2
22–23.	0.00076	97,936	74	97,898	5,315,856	54.3
23–24.	0.00082	97,861	80	97,821	5,217,958	53.3
24–25.	0.00086	97,782	84	97,739	5,120,136	52.4
25–26.	0.00091	97,697	89	97,653	5,022,397	51.4
26–27.	0.00097	97,608	95	97,561	4,924,744	50.5
27–28.	0.00104	97,514	101	97,463	4,827,184	49.5
28–29.	0.00111	97,413	108	97,358	4,729,721	48.6
29–30.	0.00120	97,304	117	97,246	4,632,362	47.6
30–31.	0.00130	97,187	126	97,124	4,535,117	46.7
31–32.	0.00140	97,061	136	96,993	4,437,993	45.7
32–33.	0.00151	96,926	147	96,852	4,340,999	44.8
33–34.	0.00165	96,779	160	96,699	4,244,147	43.9
34–35.	0.00180	96,619	174	96,532	4,147,448	42.9
35–36.	0.00196	96,445	189	96,350	4,050,917	42.0
36–37.	0.00212	96,256	204	96,154	3,954,566	41.1
37–38.	0.00229	96,052	220	95,942	3,858,413	40.2
38–39.	0.00248	95,832	238	95,713	3,762,471	39.3
39–40.	0.00270	95,594	258	95,465	3,666,758	38.4
40–41.	0.00293	95,336	279	95,196	3,571,293	37.5
41–42.	0.00316	95,057	301	94,906	3,476,097	36.6
42–43.	0.00342	94,756	324	94,594	3,381,191	35.7
43–44.	0.00369	94,432	348	94,258	3,286,597	34.8
44–45.	0.00397	94,084	374	93,897	3,192,339	33.9
45–46.	0.00430	93,710	403	93,509	3,098,442	33.1
46–47.	0.00465	93,307	434	93,091	3,004,933	32.2
47–48.	0.00499	92,874	464	92,642	2,911,843	31.4
48–49.	0.00532	92,410	492	92,164	2,819,201	30.5
49–50.	0.00565	91,918	519	91,658	2,727,037	29.7
50–51.	0.00601	91,399	549	91,124	2,635,379	28.8
51–52.	0.00643	90,850	585	90,557	2,544,254	28.0
52–53.	0.00693	90,265	626	89,952	2,453,697	27.2
53–54.	0.00751	89,639	673	89,303	2,363,745	26.4
54–55.	0.00815	88,966	725	88,604	2,274,442	25.6
55–56.	0.00884	88,241	780	87,851	2,185,838	24.8
56–57.	0.00959	87,461	839	87,042	2,097,987	24.0
57–58.	0.01039	86,622	900	86,172	2,010,945	23.2
58–59.	0.01126	85,722	965	85,240	1,924,773	22.5
59–60.	0.01220	84,757	1,034	84,240	1,839,533	21.7
60–61.	0.01324	83,723	1,109	83,169	1,755,293	21.0
61–62.	0.01435	82,615	1,185	82,022	1,672,124	20.2
62–63.	0.01544	81,429	1,257	80,800	1,590,103	19.5
63–64.	0.01645	80,172	1,319	79,512	1,509,302	18.8
64–65.	0.01741	78,853	1,373	78,167	1,429,790	18.1
65–66.	0.01828	77,480	1,416	76,772	1,351,623	17.4
66–67.	0.01925	76,064	1,465	75,332	1,274,851	16.8

Table 9. Life table for black females: United States, 1998—Con.

Age	Proportion dying during age interval	Number living at beginning of age interval	Number dying during age interval	Stationary population in the age interval	Stationary population in this and all subsequent age intervals	Life expectancy at beginning of age interval
	q_x	l_x	d_x	L_x	T_x	e_x
67–68	0.02065	74,599	1,541	73,829	1,199,519	16.1
68–69	0.02271	73,059	1,659	72,229	1,125,690	15.4
69–70	0.02536	71,400	1,811	70,494	1,053,461	14.8
70–71	0.02847	69,589	1,981	68,598	982,967	14.1
71–72	0.03166	67,608	2,141	66,538	914,368	13.5
72–73	0.03467	65,467	2,270	64,332	847,831	13.0
73–74	0.03716	63,197	2,348	62,023	783,498	12.4
74–75	0.03919	60,849	2,385	59,657	721,475	11.9
75–76	0.04110	58,464	2,403	57,263	661,819	11.3
76–77	0.04332	56,062	2,428	54,847	604,556	10.8
77–78	0.04607	53,633	2,471	52,398	549,708	10.2
78–79	0.04979	51,162	2,547	49,888	497,311	9.7
79–80	0.05455	48,615	2,652	47,289	447,422	9.2
80–81	0.06015	45,963	2,765	44,581	400,133	8.7
81–82	0.06629	43,199	2,864	41,767	355,553	8.2
82–83	0.07306	40,335	2,947	38,862	313,786	7.8
83–84	0.08012	37,388	2,996	35,890	274,924	7.4
84–85	0.08737	34,393	3,005	32,890	239,034	7.0
85–86	0.09489	31,388	2,978	29,899	206,144	6.6
86–87	0.10290	28,409	2,923	26,948	176,245	6.2
87–88	0.11142	25,486	2,840	24,066	149,297	5.9
88–89	0.12047	22,646	2,728	21,282	125,231	5.5
89–90	0.13005	19,918	2,590	18,623	103,949	5.2
90–91	0.14019	17,328	2,429	16,113	85,326	4.9
91–92	0.15089	14,899	2,248	13,775	69,213	4.6
92–93	0.16215	12,651	2,051	11,625	55,438	4.4
93–94	0.17400	10,599	1,844	9,677	43,813	4.1
94–95	0.18643	8,755	1,632	7,939	34,136	3.9
95–96	0.19944	7,123	1,421	6,412	26,197	3.7
96–97	0.21305	5,702	1,215	5,095	19,785	3.5
97–98	0.22724	4,487	1,020	3,978	14,690	3.3
98–99	0.24200	3,468	839	3,048	10,713	3.1
99–100	0.25734	2,628	676	2,290	7,665	2.9
100+	1.00000	1,952	1,952	5,374	5,374	2.8

Table 10. Survivorship by age, race, and sex: Death-registration States, 1900–1902 to 1919–21, and United States, 1929–31 to 1998

[Alaska and Hawaii included beginning in 1959. For decennial periods prior to 1929–31, data are for groups of registration States as follows: 1900–1902 and 1909–11, 10 States and the District of Columbia; 1919–21, 34 States and the District of Columbia. Beginning 1970 excludes deaths of nonresidents of the United States; see Technical notes]

Age, race, and sex	Number of survivors out of 100,000 born alive (l_x)										
	1998	1989–91	1979–81	1969–71	1959–61	1949–51	1939–41	1929–31	1919–21	1909–11	1900–1902
All races											
0	100,000	100,000	100,000	100,000	100,000	100,000	100,000	100,000	100,000	100,000	100,000
1	99,279	99,064	98,740	97,998	97,407	97,024	95,290	94,028	92,515	88,538	87,552
5	99,141	98,877	98,495	97,668	96,998	96,482	94,220	91,978	83,389	83,887	81,804
10	99,053	98,766	98,347	97,460	96,765	96,177	93,710	91,106	88,129	82,458	80,052
15	98,944	98,635	98,196	97,261	96,551	95,885	93,235	90,385	87,144	81,506	78,963
20	98,595	98,215	97,741	96,716	96,111	95,366	92,435	89,089	85,441	80,074	77,239
25	98,126	97,671	97,110	96,000	95,517	94,676	91,335	87,269	83,146	78,046	74,768
30	97,648	97,070	96,477	95,307	94,905	93,919	90,078	85,302	80,642	75,779	72,043
35	97,062	96,322	95,808	94,482	94,144	92,976	88,573	83,118	77,961	73,127	69,078
40	96,267	95,373	94,926	93,322	93,064	91,648	86,650	80,557	75,114	70,042	65,890
45	95,135	94,154	93,599	91,587	91,378	89,634	84,069	77,343	72,036	66,561	62,436
50	93,491	92,370	91,526	88,972	88,756	86,591	80,487	73,321	68,429	62,460	58,514
55	91,094	89,658	88,348	85,110	84,711	82,176	75,557	68,182	63,947	57,555	53,852
60	87,442	85,537	83,726	79,529	79,067	75,921	68,924	61,563	58,079	51,138	47,946
65	81,931	79,519	77,107	71,933	71,147	67,555	60,366	53,195	50,560	43,194	40,911
70	74,199	71,357	68,248	61,984	60,857	56,987	49,655	42,768	41,090	33,816	32,390
75	63,634	60,449	56,799	49,705	48,170	43,903	36,735	30,789	29,729	23,552	22,960
80	50,523	47,084	43,180	35,285	33,576	29,313	22,883	18,580	18,298	13,712	13,529
85	34,537	31,770	27,960	20,908	18,542	15,785	11,073	8,542	8,683	6,001	6,053
90	18,614	17,046	14,154	9,297	7,080	6,144	3,796	2,998	2,941	1,868	1,867
95	7,166	6,282	5,043	2,786	1,524	1,511	857	636	646	361	344
100	1,761	1,424	1,150	542	183	199	123	62	67	40	31
Male											
0	100,000	100,000	100,000	100,000	100,000	100,000	100,000	100,000	100,000	100,000	100,000
1	99,215	98,961	98,607	97,755	97,087	96,661	94,762	93,440	91,745	87,505	86,426
5	99,066	98,754	98,333	97,395	96,643	96,077	93,624	91,294	88,505	82,718	80,548
10	98,967	98,627	98,160	97,151	96,375	95,726	93,054	90,346	87,184	81,249	78,775
15	98,834	98,464	97,972	96,904	96,107	95,366	92,508	89,561	86,156	80,261	77,681
20	98,346	97,854	97,316	96,126	95,491	94,695	91,617	88,220	84,440	78,792	75,984
25	97,648	97,049	96,361	95,040	94,631	93,791	90,385	86,359	82,252	76,675	73,472
30	96,970	96,166	95,430	94,072	93,826	92,861	89,009	84,346	79,890	74,378	70,747
35	96,184	95,091	94,501	92,997	92,889	91,760	87,371	82,075	77,514	71,614	67,752
40	95,163	93,761	93,345	91,541	91,572	90,207	85,246	79,357	74,432	68,297	64,447
45	93,717	92,139	91,649	89,369	89,492	87,819	82,336	75,882	71,244	64,518	60,849
50	91,616	89,865	89,007	86,070	86,199	84,158	78,254	71,518	67,553	60,118	56,736
55	88,646	86,492	84,936	81,139	81,039	78,781	72,627	65,981	62,965	54,970	51,939
60	84,188	81,378	79,012	73,958	73,887	71,246	65,142	58,909	56,917	48,343	45,895
65	77,547	73,971	70,646	64,318	64,177	61,566	55,776	50,154	49,218	40,264	38,736
70	68,375	64,107	59,681	52,296	52,244	49,950	44,588	39,516	39,668	31,023	30,217
75	56,288	51,385	46,272	38,797	38,950	36,756	31,864	27,718	28,316	21,213	21,076
80	42,127	36,749	31,810	24,921	25,300	25,237	18,995	16,172	17,128	11,942	12,084
85	26,219	21,815	18,020	13,168	12,845	11,750	8,693	7,107	7,920	5,059	5,179
90	12,310	9,878	7,732	5,107	4,609	4,197	2,787	2,283	2,527	1,502	1,508
95	3,910	2,927	2,279	1,326	970	955	586	451	556	289	262
100	757	529	423	222	117	121	78	40	62	33	22
Female											
0	100,000	100,000	100,000	100,000	100,000	100,000	100,000	100,000	100,000	100,000	100,000
1	99,345	99,172	98,880	98,254	97,744	97,406	95,848	94,728	93,383	89,623	88,733
5	99,220	99,006	98,666	97,955	97,371	96,908	94,848	92,789	90,380	85,117	83,119
10	99,144	98,911	98,544	97,784	97,173	96,652	94,402	92,008	89,186	83,728	81,390
15	99,059	98,814	98,432	97,636	97,016	96,431	94,000	91,364	88,247	82,813	80,307
20	98,857	98,597	98,184	97,331	96,756	96,066	93,293	90,116	86,556	81,418	78,555
25	98,627	98,325	97,883	96,966	96,418	95,583	92,322	88,328	84,135	79,481	76,119
30	98,350	98,013	97,551	96,544	95,996	94,933	91,182	86,398	81,463	77,247	73,394
35	97,964	97,596	97,140	95,966	95,409	94,206	89,810	84,304	78,713	74,719	70,463
40	97,398	97,033	96,531	95,097	94,560	93,101	88,092	81,927	75,907	71,894	67,407
45	96,582	96,222	95,570	93,793	93,265	91,469	85,856	79,041	72,954	68,755	64,121
50	95,392	94,932	94,060	91,852	91,327	89,075	82,828	75,456	69,452	65,001	60,415
55	93,562	92,881	91,760	89,066	88,451	85,694	78,708	70,832	65,099	60,392	55,908

See footnotes at end of table.

Table 10. Survivorship by age, race, and sex: Death-registration States, 1900–1902 to 1919–21, and United States, 1929–31 to 1998—Con.

[Alaska and Hawaii included beginning in 1959. For decennial periods prior to 1929–31, data are for groups of registration States as follows: 1900–1902 and 1909–11, 10 States and the District of Columbia; 1919–21, 34 States and the District of Columbia. Beginning 1970 excludes deaths of nonresidents of the United States; see Technical notes]

Age, race, and sex	Number of survivors out of 100,000 born alive (l_x)										
	1998	1989–91	1979–81	1969–71	1959–61	1949–51	1939–41	1929–31	1919–21	1909–11	1900–1902
Female—Con.											
60	90,700	89,742	88,414	85,139	84,430	80,890	73,093	64,795	59,438	54,226	50,155
65	86,288	85,075	83,520	79,698	78,462	74,119	65,523	56,924	52,126	46,438	43,246
70	79,926	78,522	76,720	71,955	70,100	64,873	55,449	46,774	42,741	36,916	34,721
75	70,761	69,287	67,186	61,107	58,394	52,111	42,425	34,600	31,344	26,155	24,994
80	58,573	56,986	54,372	46,445	43,063	36,486	27,524	21,578	19,613	15,682	15,129
85	42,297	41,115	37,772	29,538	25,269	20,668	13,972	10,322	9,515	7,051	7,063
90	24,214	23,666	20,578	14,160	10,056	8,548	5,044	3,656	3,314	2,269	2,306
95	9,911	9,346	7,862	4,565	2,193	2,207	1,195	807	728	441	452
100	2,594	2,251	1,927	954	264	298	179	82	72	49	43
White											
0	100,000	100,000	100,000	100,000	100,000	100,000	100,000	100,000	100,000	100,000	100,000
1	99,404	99,233	98,898	98,224	97,714	97,278	95,685	94,392	92,780	88,709	87,762
5	99,284	99,068	98,675	97,930	97,353	96,790	94,713	92,466	89,771	84,147	82,071
10	99,206	98,966	98,536	97,733	97,131	96,502	94,228	91,627	88,536	82,734	80,371
15	99,103	98,843	98,391	97,546	96,928	96,228	93,792	90,982	87,633	81,816	79,344
20	98,773	98,455	97,939	97,036	96,508	95,763	93,117	89,933	86,159	80,407	77,998
25	98,354	97,972	97,340	96,406	95,965	95,169	92,213	88,454	84,106	78,392	75,202
30	97,936	97,451	96,774	95,824	95,440	94,536	91,185	86,836	81,787	76,167	72,317
35	97,418	96,810	96,192	95,152	94,798	93,750	89,941	85,004	79,277	73,568	69,522
40	96,707	96,000	95,427	94,190	93,870	92,616	88,318	82,803	76,642	70,525	66,082
45	95,698	94,932	94,257	92,681	92,374	90,847	86,069	79,989	73,705	67,090	62,920
50	94,228	93,326	92,384	90,306	89,958	88,110	82,833	76,340	70,250	62,994	58,647
55	92,021	90,833	89,427	86,688	86,173	84,027	78,218	71,551	65,875	58,163	54,450
60	88,582	86,943	85,031	81,323	80,811	78,066	71,785	65,100	60,013	51,822	48,288
65	83,280	81,123	78,585	73,889	73,102	69,850	63,201	56,655	52,411	43,904	41,505
70	75,618	73,106	69,801	63,991	62,834	59,189	52,165	45,841	42,736	34,484	32,902
75	65,079	62,175	58,299	51,586	49,895	45,688	38,610	33,406	31,086	24,151	23,356
80	51,807	48,583	44,409	36,659	34,697	30,438	23,976	20,260	19,149	14,100	13,794
85	35,463	32,850	28,768	21,578	19,017	16,239	11,483	9,325	9,078	6,178	6,192
90	19,055	17,571	14,471	9,433	7,149	6,201	3,819	3,066	2,991	1,918	1,919
95	7,160	6,416	5,067	2,743	1,521	1,500	801	636	643	364	355
100	1,609	1,423	1,105	487	183	196	98	58	62	38	31
White male											
0	100,000	100,000	100,000	100,000	100,000	100,000	100,000	100,000	100,000	100,000	100,000
1	99,352	99,138	98,769	97,994	97,408	96,931	95,188	93,768	91,975	87,674	86,655
5	99,222	98,956	98,519	97,671	97,015	96,403	94,150	91,738	88,842	82,972	80,864
10	99,134	98,839	98,357	97,441	96,758	96,069	93,601	90,810	87,530	81,519	79,109
15	99,012	98,686	98,176	97,208	96,503	95,728	93,089	90,074	86,546	80,549	78,037
20	98,563	98,134	97,525	96,480	95,908	95,104	92,293	88,904	84,997	79,116	76,376
25	97,942	97,430	96,616	95,524	95,106	94,294	91,241	87,371	83,061	77,047	73,907
30	97,348	96,662	95,783	94,716	94,401	93,489	90,092	85,707	80,888	74,810	71,219
35	96,646	95,731	94,980	93,843	93,589	92,543	88,713	83,812	78,441	72,108	68,245
40	95,722	94,588	93,984	92,631	92,427	91,173	86,880	81,457	75,733	68,848	64,954
45	94,414	93,167	92,494	90,725	90,533	89,002	84,285	78,345	72,696	65,115	61,369
50	92,528	91,124	90,105	87,690	87,424	85,601	80,521	74,288	69,107	60,741	57,274
55	89,800	88,022	86,303	83,001	82,463	80,496	75,156	68,981	64,574	55,622	52,491
60	85,600	83,182	80,625	75,969	75,485	73,172	67,787	61,933	58,498	48,987	46,452
65	79,211	75,962	72,393	66,343	65,834	63,541	58,305	52,964	50,663	40,862	39,245
70	70,065	66,181	61,384	54,138	53,825	51,735	46,739	41,880	40,873	31,527	30,640
75	57,899	53,308	47,712	40,324	40,207	38,104	33,404	29,471	29,205	21,585	21,387
80	43,462	38,245	32,788	25,885	25,993	24,005	19,860	17,221	17,655	12,160	12,266
85	27,058	22,720	18,538	13,527	13,065	12,015	9,013	7,572	8,154	5,145	5,252
90	12,620	10,214	7,891	5,125	4,600	4,209	2,812	2,356	2,568	1,523	1,523
95	3,881	2,988	2,279	1,274	956	942	552	461	556	289	263
100	681	523	404	189	115	118	65	40	61	31	22

See footnotes at end of table.

Table 10. Survivorship by age, race, and sex: Death-registration States, 1900–1902 to 1919–21, and United States, 1929–31 to 1998—Con.

[Alaska and Hawaii included beginning in 1959. For decennial periods prior to 1929–31, data are for groups of registration States as follows: 1900–1902 and 1909–11, 10 States and the District of Columbia; 1919–21, 34 States and the District of Columbia. Beginning 1970 excludes deaths of nonresidents of the United States; see Technical notes]

Age, race, and sex	Number of survivors out of 100,000 born alive (l_x)										
	1998	1989–91	1979–81	1969–71	1959–61	1949–51	1939–41	1929–31	1919–21	1909–11	1900–1902
White female											
0	100,000	100,000	100,000	100,000	100,000	100,000	100,000	100,000	100,000	100,000	100,000
1	99,458	99,333	99,035	98,468	98,036	97,645	96,211	95,037	93,608	89,774	88,939
5	99,348	99,187	98,841	98,203	97,709	97,199	95,309	93,216	90,721	85,349	83,426
10	99,281	99,099	98,725	98,042	97,525	96,960	94,890	92,466	89,564	83,979	81,723
15	99,199	99,007	98,618	97,902	97,375	96,756	94,534	91,894	88,712	83,093	80,680
20	98,995	98,795	98,374	97,618	97,135	96,454	93,984	90,939	87,281	81,750	78,978
25	98,791	98,547	98,093	97,299	96,844	96,072	93,228	89,524	85,163	79,865	76,588
30	98,553	98,283	97,802	96,945	96,499	95,605	92,320	87,972	82,740	77,676	73,887
35	98,221	97,939	97,445	96,474	96,026	94,977	91,211	86,248	80,206	75,200	70,971
40	97,731	97,472	96,913	95,762	95,326	94,080	89,805	84,256	77,624	72,425	67,935
45	97,027	96,768	96,065	94,649	94,228	92,725	87,920	81,780	74,871	69,341	64,677
50	95,981	95,608	94,710	92,924	92,522	90,685	85,267	78,572	71,547	65,629	61,005
55	94,298	93,730	92,594	90,383	89,967	87,699	81,520	74,321	67,323	61,053	56,509
60	91,616	90,789	89,451	86,726	86,339	83,279	76,200	68,462	61,704	54,900	50,752
65	87,390	86,339	84,764	81,579	80,739	76,773	68,701	60,499	54,299	47,086	43,806
70	81,151	79,984	78,139	74,101	72,507	67,545	58,363	49,932	44,638	37,482	35,206
75	72,110	70,834	68,712	63,290	60,461	54,397	44,685	37,024	32,777	26,569	25,362
80	59,852	58,454	55,770	48,182	44,676	38,026	28,882	23,053	20,492	15,929	15,349
85	43,316	42,274	38,774	30,490	26,046	21,348	14,487	10,937	9,909	7,152	7,149
90	24,761	24,270	20,996	14,406	10,219	8,662	5,061	3,719	3,372	2,291	2,322
95	9,906	9,495	7,900	4,526	2,203	2,200	1,109	797	721	434	448
100	2,361	2,239	1,858	872	265	294	139	74	63	44	41
Black[1]											
0	100,000	100,000	100,000	100,000	100,000	100,000	100,000	100,000	100,000	100,000	100,000
1	98,566	98,187	97,885	96,731	95,732	95,407	92,584	92,035	90,379	79,784	76,609
5	98,323	97,884	97,522	96,207	95,051	94,482	90,983	89,303	86,174	70,691	66,222
10	98,180	97,720	97,322	95,928	94,745	94,060	90,339	88,258	84,690	68,437	63,410
15	98,033	97,539	97,134	95,661	94,460	93,646	89,591	87,156	83,180	66,410	61,060
20	97,556	96,925	96,652	94,887	93,880	92,738	87,839	84,386	79,641	63,165	57,931
25	96,775	95,972	95,804	93,513	92,925	91,321	85,210	80,320	74,973	59,608	54,512
30	95,904	94,809	94,680	91,934	91,699	89,584	82,194	75,962	70,492	56,112	51,287
35	94,846	93,260	93,288	89,977	90,046	87,402	78,683	71,141	65,865	52,125	48,007
40	93,403	91,239	91,439	87,304	87,766	84,478	74,466	65,974	61,244	47,866	44,518
45	91,293	88,689	88,834	83,700	84,501	80,507	69,284	59,827	56,442	43,054	40,628
50	88,174	85,285	85,044	78,938	80,172	74,976	62,702	53,141	51,422	37,800	36,103
55	83,958	80,635	79,816	72,826	73,893	67,660	54,846	45,558	45,803	32,233	31,404
60	78,210	74,335	72,913	65,250	65,795	58,593	46,318	37,654	39,418	26,046	25,698
65	70,516	66,154	64,391	56,102	56,038	48,649	37,838	30,015	32,738	19,806	20,474
70	61,604	56,192	54,617	45,785	45,434	38,616	29,654	22,505	25,585	14,021	14,960
75	49,915	44,872	43,274	34,262	34,531	28,968	21,798	15,546	18,011	9,139	9,956
80	37,463	33,149	31,711	23,710	24,815	20,003	14,408	9,589	11,376	5,158	5,750
85	24,189	21,352	19,939	15,044	15,337	12,433	8,326	4,900	5,794	2,414	2,782
90	12,647	11,646	10,713	8,087	7,195	6,394	4,077	2,044	2,317	913	1,054
95	4,995	4,729	4,463	3,252	1,777	2,010	1,557	638	689	324	296
100	1,351	1,376	1,360	1,036	214	301	399	120	129	77	57
Black male[1]											
0	100,000	100,000	100,000	100,000	100,000	100,000	100,000	100,000	100,000	100,000	100,000
1	98,421	98,023	97,703	96,394	95,301	94,911	91,772	91,268	89,499	78,065	74,674
5	98,149	97,688	97,300	95,826	94,570	93,921	90,082	88,412	85,195	68,589	64,385
10	97,986	97,501	97,061	95,497	94,234	93,453	89,393	87,311	83,768	66,377	61,730
15	97,799	97,268	96,826	95,161	93,874	92,965	88,610	86,152	82,332	64,478	59,667
20	97,068	96,301	96,132	94,053	93,108	91,941	86,968	83,621	79,057	61,426	56,733
25	95,867	94,809	94,827	91,904	91,825	90,285	84,227	79,516	74,540	57,736	53,285
30	94,609	93,070	93,125	89,584	90,270	88,327	80,979	75,083	70,344	54,073	49,867
35	93,203	90,827	91,080	86,885	88,331	85,940	77,221	70,049	65,873	49,865	46,541
40	91,396	87,948	88,490	83,441	85,744	82,832	72,780	64,710	61,353	45,414	42,989
45	88,757	84,467	84,997	78,976	82,075	78,686	67,346	58,432	56,589	40,563	39,230
50	84,731	79,984	80,065	73,282	77,239	72,891	60,495	51,748	51,880	35,427	34,766
55	79,315	74,095	73,413	66,101	70,351	65,122	52,426	44,436	46,581	29,754	29,987

See footnotes at end of table.

Table 10. Survivorship by age, race, and sex: Death-registration States, 1900–1902 to 1919–21, and United States, 1929–31 to 1998—Con.

[Alaska and Hawaii included beginning in 1959. For decennial periods prior to 1929–31, data are for groups of registration States as follows: 1900–1902 and 1909–11, 10 States and the District of Columbia; 1919–21, 34 States and the District of Columbia. Beginning 1970 excludes deaths of nonresidents of the United States; see Technical notes]

Age, race, and sex	Number of survivors out of 100,000 born alive (l_x)										
	1998	1989–91	1979–81	1969–71	1959–61	1949–51	1939–41	1929–31	1919–21	1909–11	1900–1902
Black male[1]—Con.											
60	72,158	66,334	64,980	57,457	61,669	55,535	43,833	36,790	40,506	23,750	24,194
65	62,829	56,795	55,061	47,485	51,392	45,198	35,371	29,314	34,042	17,806	19,015
70	52,886	45,690	44,213	36,925	39,914	35,018	27,236	21,741	26,923	12,295	13,829
75	40,667	33,755	32,717	25,921	29,064	25,472	19,456	14,419	18,854	7,494	8,892
80	28,375	22,549	22,017	16,560	19,994	16,904	12,186	8,239	11,615	3,894	4,831
85	16,434	12,709	12,383	9,648	11,620	9,898	6,444	3,660	5,605	1,747	2,030
90	7,494	5,972	5,708	4,696	5,174	4,642	2,836	1,246	2,040	595	634
95	2,546	1,971	2,009	1,721	1,240	1,342	961	307	552	189	137
100	607	466	513	489	149	192	209	41	77	40	18
Black female[1]											
0	100,000	100,000	100,000	100,000	100,000	100,000	100,000	100,000	100,000	100,000	100,000
1	98,715	98,356	98,073	97,076	96,172	95,913	93,416	92,796	91,251	81,493	78,525
5	98,503	98,087	97,751	96,598	95,543	95,055	91,906	90,185	87,149	72,768	68,056
10	98,380	97,946	97,590	96,369	95,265	94,679	91,308	89,201	85,607	70,508	65,111
15	98,276	97,818	97,450	96,172	95,057	94,343	90,594	88,088	83,954	68,218	62,384
20	98,063	97,566	97,180	95,729	94,660	93,544	88,736	85,078	80,154	64,764	59,053
25	97,697	97,140	96,754	95,035	94,005	92,336	86,198	81,067	75,359	61,430	55,795
30	97,187	96,514	96,150	94,114	93,070	90,799	83,384	76,816	70,633	58,281	52,773
35	96,445	95,599	95,338	92,807	91,670	88,805	80,092	72,192	65,857	54,595	49,567
40	95,336	94,364	94,137	90,817	89,676	86,052	76,084	67,271	61,130	50,568	46,146
45	93,710	92,676	92,322	88,001	86,793	82,257	71,157	61,365	56,230	45,947	42,279
50	91,399	90,277	89,563	84,168	82,979	77,007	64,885	54,920	50,780	40,886	37,681
55	88,241	86,793	85,653	79,177	77,362	70,196	57,314	47,074	44,742	35,415	33,124
60	83,723	81,886	80,293	72,820	69,941	61,758	48,928	38,761	37,954	28,908	27,524
65	77,480	75,031	73,266	64,716	60,825	52,358	40,504	30,852	31,044	22,302	21,995
70	69,589	66,278	64,729	54,873	51,274	42,612	32,354	23,341	24,107	15,871	16,140
75	58,464	55,684	53,831	43,193	40,540	32,981	24,502	16,576	17,216	10,657	11,066
80	45,963	43,622	41,686	31,756	30,315	23,712	17,039	10,822	11,151	6,324	6,708
85	31,388	30,089	28,004	21,358	19,744	15,550	10,622	6,033	5,972	3,029	3,567
90	17,328	17,536	16,260	12,210	9,675	8,590	5,652	2,774	2,579	1,206	1,492
95	7,123	7,687	7,312	5,217	2,438	2,875	2,345	941	818	448	462
100	1,952	2,364	2,398	1,803	293	445	659	193	179	112	97

[1]For 1939–41 and 1949–51, data shown are for the entire nonwhite population. During these periods, life tables were not constructed for the black population. See Technical notes.

Table 11. Life expectancy by age, race, and sex: Death-registration States, 1900–1902 to 1919–21, and United States, 1929–31 to 1998

[Alaska and Hawaii included beginning in 1959. For decennial periods prior to 1929–31, data are for groups of registration States as follows: 1900–1902 and 1909–11, 10 States and the District of Columbia; 1919–21, 34 States and the District of Columbia. Beginning 1970 excludes deaths of nonresidents of the United States; see Technical notes]

Age, race, and sex	Average number of years of life remaining (e_x)										
	1998	1989–91	1979–81	1969–71	1959–61	1949–51	1939–41	1929–31	1919–21	1909–11	1900–1902
All races											
0	76.7	75.37	73.88	70.75	69.89	68.07	63.62	59.20	56.40	51.49	49.24
1	76.3	75.08	73.82	71.19	70.75	69.16	65.76	61.94	59.94	57.11	55.20
5	72.4	71.22	70.00	67.43	67.04	65.54	62.49	59.29	57.99	56.21	54.98
10	67.4	66.29	65.10	62.57	62.19	60.74	57.82	54.84	53.79	52.15	51.14
15	62.5	61.38	60.19	57.69	57.33	55.91	53.10	50.25	49.37	47.73	46.81
20	57.7	56.63	55.46	53.00	52.58	51.20	48.54	45.94	45.30	43.53	42.79
25	53.0	51.93	50.81	48.37	47.89	46.56	44.09	41.85	41.47	39.60	39.12
30	48.2	47.23	46.12	43.71	43.18	41.91	39.67	37.75	37.68	35.70	35.51
35	43.5	42.58	41.43	39.07	38.51	37.31	35.30	33.68	33.89	31.90	31.92
40	38.8	37.98	36.79	34.52	33.92	32.81	31.03	29.67	30.08	28.20	28.34
45	34.3	33.44	32.27	30.12	29.50	28.49	26.90	25.79	26.25	24.54	24.77
50	29.8	29.03	27.94	25.93	25.29	24.40	22.98	22.06	22.50	20.98	21.26
55	25.5	24.83	23.85	21.99	21.37	20.57	19.31	18.53	18.90	17.55	17.88
60	21.5	20.90	20.02	18.34	17.71	17.04	15.91	15.24	15.54	14.42	14.76
65	17.8	17.28	16.51	15.00	14.39	13.83	12.80	12.23	12.47	11.60	11.86
70	14.3	13.96	13.32	12.00	11.38	10.92	10.00	9.58	9.74	9.11	9.30
75	11.3	11.00	10.48	9.32	8.71	8.40	7.62	7.32	7.49	6.99	7.08
80	8.6	8.40	7.98	7.10	6.39	6.34	5.73	5.50	5.63	5.25	5.30
85	6.3	6.23	5.96	5.28	4.58	4.69	4.31	4.19	4.21	4.00	3.96
90	4.7	4.50	4.43	3.94	3.22	3.44	3.30	3.15	3.22	3.03	2.95
95	3.5	3.29	3.34	3.06	2.43	2.54	2.61	2.26	2.32	2.35	2.18
100	2.6	2.46	2.73	2.62	1.91	1.92	2.13	1.51	1.53	1.85	1.58
Male											
0	73.8	71.83	70.11	67.04	66.80	65.47	61.60	57.71	55.50	49.86	47.88
1	73.4	71.58	70.10	67.58	67.80	66.73	64.00	60.75	59.47	55.95	54.35
5	69.5	67.73	66.29	63.82	64.10	63.12	60.76	58.14	57.60	55.11	54.22
10	64.6	62.81	61.41	58.98	59.27	58.35	56.12	53.75	53.44	51.07	50.39
15	59.7	57.91	56.52	54.12	54.43	53.56	51.43	49.18	49.05	46.66	46.06
20	55.0	53.25	51.88	49.54	49.77	48.92	46.91	44.88	44.99	42.48	42.03
25	50.3	48.67	47.37	45.07	45.19	44.36	42.51	40.79	41.11	38.59	38.38
30	45.7	44.10	42.81	40.51	40.56	39.78	38.13	36.71	37.26	34.70	34.76
35	41.0	39.57	38.20	35.95	35.94	35.23	33.79	32.65	33.43	30.94	31.19
40	36.4	35.09	33.64	31.48	31.42	30.79	29.57	28.68	29.63	27.32	27.65
45	31.9	30.66	29.22	27.18	27.09	26.55	25.52	24.87	25.84	23.77	24.14
50	27.6	26.37	25.00	23.12	23.02	22.59	21.72	21.25	22.11	20.32	20.70
55	23.5	22.30	21.08	19.36	19.32	18.96	18.20	17.79	18.53	16.98	17.38
60	19.6	18.53	17.46	15.99	15.94	15.68	14.99	14.62	15.22	13.95	14.33
65	16.0	15.12	14.21	12.99	12.95	12.74	12.07	11.72	12.20	11.24	11.50
70	12.8	12.05	11.35	10.39	10.33	10.11	9.46	9.18	9.52	8.83	9.02
75	10.0	9.39	8.90	8.13	7.99	7.83	7.22	7.02	7.31	6.75	6.84
80	7.5	7.12	6.80	6.27	5.95	5.94	5.44	5.27	5.49	5.10	5.11
85	5.5	5.31	5.13	4.73	4.39	4.41	4.11	4.02	4.10	3.90	3.82
90	4.1	3.89	3.89	3.60	3.18	3.30	3.17	3.06	3.21	3.01	2.86
95	3.0	2.92	2.98	2.82	2.43	2.49	2.52	2.21	2.38	2.36	2.13
100	2.3	2.25	2.49	2.43	1.91	1.92	2.05	1.50	1.58	1.81	1.55
Female											
0	79.5	78.81	77.62	74.64	73.24	70.96	65.89	60.90	57.40	53.24	50.70
1	79.0	78.47	77.50	74.97	73.93	71.84	67.73	65.37	60.45	58.37	56.10
5	75.1	74.60	73.67	71.19	70.21	68.21	64.43	60.66	58.41	57.39	55.80
10	70.2	69.67	68.75	66.31	65.35	63.38	59.73	56.16	54.16	53.31	51.94
15	65.2	64.73	63.83	61.41	60.45	58.52	54.97	51.54	49.71	48.87	47.60
20	60.3	59.87	58.98	56.59	55.60	53.73	50.37	47.21	45.63	44.66	43.60
25	55.5	55.03	54.16	51.80	50.79	48.99	45.87	43.11	41.86	40.69	39.92
30	50.6	50.19	49.33	47.01	46.00	44.28	41.41	39.02	38.15	36.79	36.30
35	45.8	45.40	44.53	42.28	41.27	39.63	37.01	34.92	34.40	32.95	32.71
40	41.1	40.65	39.80	37.64	36.61	35.06	32.68	30.86	30.58	29.15	29.08
45	36.4	35.97	35.17	33.13	32.09	30.64	28.46	26.89	26.71	25.36	25.44
50	31.8	31.42	30.69	28.77	27.71	26.40	24.40	23.05	22.92	21.67	21.84
55	27.4	27.05	26.39	24.59	23.53	22.33	20.54	19.38	19.28	18.13	18.39

See footnotes at end of table.

Table 11. Life expectancy by age, race, and sex: Death-registration States, 1900–1902 to 1919–21, and United States, 1929–31 to 1998—Con.

[Alaska and Hawaii included beginning in 1959. For decennial periods prior to 1929–31, data are for groups of registration States as follows: 1900–1902 and 1909–11, 10 States and the District of Columbia; 1919–21, 34 States and the District of Columbia. Beginning 1970 excludes deaths of nonresidents of the United States; see Technical notes]

Age, race, and sex	Average number of years of life remaining (e_x)										
	1998	1989–91	1979–81	1969–71	1959–61	1949–51	1939–41	1929–31	1919–21	1909–11	1900–1902
Female—Con.											
60	23.2	22.90	22.29	20.60	19.52	18.50	16.92	15.94	15.87	14.90	15.21
65	19.2	19.02	18.44	16.83	15.80	14.95	13.57	12.78	12.73	11.96	12.22
70	15.5	15.38	14.84	13.35	12.37	11.71	10.56	9.99	9.96	9.38	9.59
75	12.2	12.08	11.58	10.26	9.33	8.94	8.01	7.61	7.65	7.20	7.34
80	9.2	9.13	8.69	7.68	6.72	6.67	5.99	5.70	5.75	5.37	5.51
85	6.7	6.66	6.38	5.63	4.71	4.90	4.47	4.32	4.30	4.08	4.12
90	4.9	4.73	4.66	4.14	3.25	3.54	3.39	3.24	3.23	3.05	3.04
95	3.6	3.40	3.48	3.18	2.43	2.57	2.67	2.30	2.27	2.34	2.24
100	2.7	2.52	2.81	2.69	1.91	1.93	2.17	1.52	1.48	1.91	1.61
White											
0	77.3	76.13	74.53	71.62	70.73	69.02	64.92	60.86	57.42	51.90	49.64
1	76.8	75.72	74.35	71.91	71.38	69.95	66.84	63.46	60.87	57.46	55.47
5	72.9	71.84	70.52	68.12	67.64	66.29	63.52	60.75	58.86	56.51	55.18
10	67.9	66.92	65.62	63.26	62.79	61.48	58.83	56.29	54.65	52.43	51.34
15	63.0	61.99	60.71	58.37	57.92	56.65	54.09	51.69	50.21	48.01	47.01
20	58.2	57.23	55.98	53.66	53.16	51.91	49.47	47.28	46.04	43.77	43.17
25	53.4	52.50	51.30	49.00	48.44	47.22	44.92	43.02	42.07	39.79	39.26
30	48.6	47.76	46.59	44.28	43.69	42.52	40.40	38.76	38.17	35.86	35.51
35	43.9	43.06	41.86	39.58	38.97	37.86	35.93	34.50	34.27	32.03	32.01
40	39.2	38.41	37.17	34.95	34.33	33.29	31.54	30.33	30.38	28.29	28.28
45	34.6	33.81	32.60	30.48	29.84	28.88	27.29	26.29	26.45	24.60	24.82
50	30.1	29.34	28.21	26.21	25.57	24.70	23.26	22.42	22.64	21.01	21.18
55	25.7	25.08	24.05	22.19	21.58	20.77	19.47	18.75	18.97	17.57	17.91
60	21.6	21.08	20.16	18.48	17.84	17.15	15.98	15.37	15.57	14.43	14.73
65	17.8	17.40	16.59	15.08	14.44	13.86	12.80	12.28	12.47	11.60	11.87
70	14.4	14.02	13.35	12.01	11.37	10.89	9.96	9.58	9.72	9.10	9.31
75	11.3	11.03	10.47	9.27	8.65	8.34	7.55	7.30	7.47	6.98	7.08
80	8.5	8.39	7.95	7.01	6.33	6.27	5.64	5.45	5.59	5.22	5.30
85	6.3	6.20	5.90	5.19	4.53	4.62	4.20	4.12	4.15	3.97	3.95
90	4.5	4.46	4.36	3.84	3.20	3.41	3.16	3.10	3.17	3.00	2.93
95	3.3	3.25	3.25	2.92	2.43	2.53	2.45	2.22	2.28	2.29	2.16
100	2.4	2.43	2.62	2.41	1.91	1.92	1.95	1.48	1.50	1.71	1.56
White male											
0	74.5	72.72	70.82	67.94	67.55	66.31	62.81	59.12	56.34	50.23	48.23
1	74.0	72.35	70.70	68.33	68.34	67.41	64.98	62.04	60.24	56.26	54.61
5	70.1	68.48	66.87	64.55	64.61	63.77	61.68	59.38	58.31	55.37	54.43
10	65.2	63.55	61.98	59.69	59.78	58.98	57.03	54.96	54.15	51.32	50.59
15	60.2	58.65	57.09	54.83	54.93	54.18	52.33	50.39	49.74	46.91	46.25
20	55.5	53.96	52.45	50.22	50.25	49.52	47.76	46.02	45.60	42.71	42.19
25	50.8	49.33	47.92	45.70	45.65	44.93	43.28	41.78	41.60	38.79	38.52
30	46.1	44.71	43.31	41.07	40.97	40.29	38.80	37.54	37.65	34.87	34.88
35	41.5	40.12	38.66	36.43	36.31	35.68	34.36	33.33	33.74	31.08	31.29
40	36.8	35.57	34.04	31.87	31.73	31.17	30.03	29.22	29.86	27.43	27.74
45	32.3	31.07	29.55	27.48	27.34	26.87	25.87	25.28	26.00	23.86	24.21
50	27.9	26.71	25.26	23.34	23.22	22.83	21.96	21.51	22.22	20.39	20.76
55	23.7	22.56	21.25	19.51	19.45	19.11	18.34	17.97	18.59	17.03	17.42
60	19.7	18.71	17.56	16.07	16.01	15.76	15.05	14.72	15.25	13.98	14.35
65	16.1	15.24	14.26	13.02	12.97	12.75	12.07	11.77	12.21	11.25	11.51
70	12.8	12.11	11.35	10.38	10.29	10.07	9.42	9.20	9.51	8.83	9.03
75	10.0	9.40	8.87	8.06	7.92	7.77	7.17	7.02	7.30	6.75	6.84
80	7.5	7.11	6.76	6.18	5.89	5.88	5.38	5.26	5.47	5.09	5.10
85	5.4	5.28	5.09	4.63	4.34	4.35	4.02	3.99	4.06	3.88	3.81
90	4.0	3.85	3.83	3.49	3.16	3.27	3.06	3.03	3.18	2.99	2.85
95	2.9	2.88	2.91	2.67	2.43	2.48	2.40	2.19	2.36	2.31	2.12
100	2.2	2.21	2.41	2.20	1.91	1.92	1.96	1.49	1.58	1.68	1.55

See footnotes at end of table.

Table 11. Life expectancy by age, race, and sex: Death-registration States, 1900–1902 to 1919–21, and United States, 1929–31 to 1998—Con.

[Alaska and Hawaii included beginning in 1959. For decennial periods prior to 1929–31, data are for groups of registration States as follows: 1900–1902 and 1909–11, 10 States and the District of Columbia; 1919–21, 34 States and the District of Columbia. Beginning 1970 excludes deaths of nonresidents of the United States; see Technical notes]

Age, race, and sex	Average number of years of life remaining (e_x)										
	1998	1989–91	1979–81	1969–71	1959–61	1949–51	1939–41	1929–31	1919–21	1909–11	1900–1902
White female											
0	80.0	79.45	78.22	75.49	74.19	72.03	67.29	62.67	58.53	53.62	51.08
1	79.4	78.99	77.98	75.66	74.68	72.77	68.93	64.93	61.51	58.69	56.39
5	75.5	75.10	74.13	71.86	70.92	69.09	65.57	62.17	59.43	57.67	56.03
10	70.6	70.16	69.21	66.97	66.05	64.26	60.85	57.65	55.17	53.57	52.15
15	65.6	65.23	64.29	62.07	61.15	59.39	56.07	53.00	50.67	49.12	47.79
20	60.8	60.36	59.44	57.24	56.29	54.56	51.38	48.52	46.46	44.88	43.77
25	55.9	55.51	54.60	52.42	51.45	49.77	46.78	44.25	42.55	40.88	40.05
30	51.0	50.65	49.76	47.60	46.63	45.00	42.21	39.99	38.72	36.96	36.42
35	46.2	45.82	44.93	42.82	41.84	40.28	37.70	35.73	34.86	33.09	32.82
40	41.4	41.03	40.16	38.12	37.13	35.64	33.25	31.52	30.94	29.26	29.17
45	36.7	36.30	35.49	33.54	32.53	31.12	28.90	27.39	26.98	25.45	25.51
50	32.0	31.71	30.96	29.11	28.08	26.76	24.72	23.41	23.12	21.74	21.89
55	27.6	27.29	26.61	24.85	23.81	22.58	20.73	19.60	19.40	18.18	18.43
60	23.3	23.09	22.45	20.79	19.69	18.64	17.00	16.05	15.93	14.92	15.23
65	19.3	19.14	18.55	16.93	15.88	15.00	13.56	12.81	12.75	11.97	12.23
70	15.6	15.46	14.89	13.37	12.38	11.68	10.50	9.98	9.94	9.38	9.59
75	12.2	12.11	11.58	10.21	9.28	8.87	7.92	7.56	7.62	7.20	7.33
80	9.1	9.12	8.65	7.59	6.67	6.59	5.88	5.63	5.70	5.35	5.50
85	6.6	6.62	6.32	5.54	4.66	4.83	4.34	4.24	4.24	4.06	4.10
90	4.7	4.69	4.59	4.05	3.23	3.51	3.24	3.17	3.16	3.00	3.02
95	3.4	3.36	3.39	3.04	2.43	2.56	2.47	2.24	2.20	2.27	2.21
100	2.4	2.49	2.70	2.49	1.91	1.92	1.95	1.48	1.42	1.74	1.58
Black[1]											
0	71.3	69.16	68.52	64.11	63.91	60.73	53.85	48.53	47.03	35.87	33.80
1	71.4	69.43	68.99	65.27	65.75	62.65	57.15	51.71	51.01	43.84	43.00
5	67.6	65.64	65.25	61.62	62.21	59.25	54.13	49.25	49.44	45.34	45.55
10	62.6	60.75	60.38	56.79	57.41	54.50	49.50	44.80	45.26	41.74	42.46
15	57.7	55.86	55.49	51.94	52.57	49.73	44.89	40.37	41.02	38.02	39.04
20	53.0	51.19	50.75	47.34	47.88	45.19	40.73	36.62	37.72	34.86	36.03
25	48.4	46.67	46.18	43.00	43.35	40.85	36.91	33.32	34.91	31.72	33.04
30	43.8	42.22	41.69	38.70	38.89	36.59	33.17	30.07	31.98	28.43	29.96
35	39.3	37.87	37.28	34.48	34.56	32.44	29.53	26.94	29.07	25.39	26.82
40	34.9	33.65	32.98	30.46	30.39	28.48	26.06	23.82	26.07	22.41	23.73
45	30.6	29.55	28.87	26.65	26.46	24.75	22.82	20.97	23.17	19.58	20.67
50	26.6	25.62	25.03	23.11	22.74	21.38	19.94	18.22	20.17	16.84	17.95
55	22.8	21.95	21.50	19.83	19.45	18.41	17.43	15.80	17.33	14.33	15.23
60	19.3	18.59	18.29	16.83	16.53	15.87	15.18	13.62	14.72	12.16	13.06
65	16.1	15.56	15.37	14.16	13.96	13.59	13.02	11.49	12.22	10.22	10.87
70	13.0	12.87	12.67	11.77	11.63	11.48	10.93	9.54	9.90	8.59	8.96
75	10.5	10.48	10.32	9.89	9.52	9.48	8.97	7.84	8.00	7.08	7.24
80	8.2	8.30	8.17	8.20	7.28	7.62	7.31	6.19	6.22	5.80	5.79
85	6.3	6.51	6.54	6.54	5.27	5.79	5.91	4.92	4.88	4.80	4.56
90	4.8	4.94	5.13	5.09	3.48	3.97	4.64	3.83	3.84	4.26	3.60
95	3.7	3.82	4.08	4.28	2.43	2.70	3.51	2.83	2.90	3.31	2.82
100	2.8	2.91	3.58	3.93	1.91	1.94	2.57	1.87	1.94	2.27	2.18
Black male[1]											
0	67.6	64.47	64.10	60.00	61.48	58.91	52.26	47.55	47.14	34.05	32.54
1	67.7	64.76	64.60	61.24	63.50	61.06	55.93	51.08	51.63	42.53	42.46
5	63.9	60.98	60.86	57.60	59.98	57.69	52.95	48.69	50.18	44.25	45.06
10	59.0	56.09	56.01	52.79	55.19	52.96	48.34	44.27	45.99	40.65	41.90
15	54.1	51.22	51.14	47.96	50.39	48.23	43.74	39.83	41.75	36.77	38.26
20	49.5	46.71	46.48	43.49	45.78	43.73	39.52	35.95	38.36	33.46	35.11
25	45.1	42.40	42.09	39.45	41.38	39.49	35.72	32.67	35.54	30.44	32.21
30	40.6	38.14	37.81	35.40	37.05	35.31	32.05	29.45	32.51	27.33	29.25
35	36.2	34.02	33.60	31.42	32.81	31.21	28.48	26.39	29.54	24.42	26.16
40	31.9	30.05	29.51	27.61	28.72	27.29	25.06	23.36	26.53	21.57	23.12
45	27.7	26.18	25.61	24.03	24.89	23.59	21.88	20.59	23.55	18.85	20.09
50	23.9	22.50	22.03	20.69	21.28	20.25	19.06	17.92	20.47	16.21	17.34
55	20.4	19.08	18.79	17.66	18.11	17.36	16.60	15.46	17.50	13.82	14.69

See footnotes at end of table.

Table 11. Life expectancy by age, race, and sex: Death-registration States, 1900–1902 to 1919–21, and United States, 1929–31 to 1998—Con.

[Alaska and Hawaii included beginning in 1959. For decennial periods prior to 1929–31, data are for groups of registration States as follows: 1900–1902 and 1909–11, 10 States and the District of Columbia; 1919–21, 34 States and the District of Columbia. Beginning 1970 excludes deaths of nonresidents of the United States; see Technical notes]

Age, race, and sex	Average number of years of life remaining (e_x)										
	1998	1989–91	1979–81	1969–71	1959–61	1949–51	1939–41	1929–31	1919–21	1909–11	1900–1902
Black male[1]											
60	17.1	16.01	15.89	14.93	15.29	14.91	14.37	13.15	14.74	11.67	12.62
65	14.3	13.27	13.29	12.53	12.84	12.75	12.21	10.87	12.07	9.74	10.38
70	11.5	10.88	10.94	10.40	10.81	10.74	10.11	8.78	9.58	8.00	8.33
75	9.2	8.84	8.90	8.76	8.93	8.83	8.17	6.99	7.61	6.58	6.60
80	7.1	7.01	7.03	7.35	6.87	7.07	6.58	5.42	5.83	5.53	5.12
85	5.5	5.58	5.61	5.92	5.08	5.38	5.34	4.30	4.53	4.48	4.04
90	4.3	4.24	4.47	4.68	3.42	3.78	4.23	3.42	3.60	4.01	3.21
95	3.4	3.37	3.62	3.92	2.43	2.64	3.20	2.54	2.61	3.15	2.50
100	2.7	2.63	3.24	3.61	1.91	1.93	2.29	1.68	1.64	2.14	1.89
Black female[1]											
0	74.8	73.73	72.88	68.32	66.47	62.70	55.56	49.51	46.92	37.67	35.04
1	74.8	73.96	73.31	69.37	68.10	64.37	58.46	52.33	50.39	45.15	43.54
5	70.9	70.16	69.54	65.70	64.54	60.93	55.40	49.81	48.70	46.42	46.04
10	66.0	65.26	64.65	60.85	59.72	56.17	50.75	45.33	44.54	42.84	43.02
15	61.1	60.34	59.74	55.97	54.85	51.36	46.13	40.87	40.36	39.18	39.79
20	56.2	55.49	54.90	51.22	50.07	46.77	42.04	37.22	37.15	36.14	36.89
25	51.4	50.72	50.13	46.57	45.40	42.35	38.20	33.93	34.35	32.97	33.90
30	46.7	46.03	45.43	42.00	40.83	38.02	34.40	30.67	31.48	29.61	30.70
35	42.0	41.45	40.79	37.56	36.41	33.82	30.83	27.47	28.58	26.44	27.52
40	37.5	36.96	36.28	33.32	32.16	29.82	27.19	24.30	25.60	23.34	24.37
45	33.1	32.58	31.94	29.31	28.14	26.07	23.89	21.39	22.61	20.43	21.36
50	28.8	28.38	27.84	25.52	24.31	22.67	20.95	18.60	19.76	17.65	18.67
55	24.8	24.41	24.00	21.97	20.89	19.62	18.38	16.27	17.09	14.98	15.88
60	21.0	20.71	20.42	18.66	17.83	16.95	16.10	14.22	14.69	12.78	13.60
65	17.4	17.37	17.13	15.67	15.12	14.54	13.95	12.24	12.41	10.82	11.38
70	14.1	14.32	14.05	13.02	12.46	12.29	11.82	10.38	10.25	9.22	9.62
75	11.3	11.56	11.37	10.85	10.10	10.15	9.81	8.62	8.37	7.55	7.90
80	8.7	9.05	8.95	8.87	7.66	8.15	8.02	6.90	6.58	6.05	6.48
85	6.6	6.99	7.09	7.00	5.44	6.15	6.41	5.48	5.22	5.09	5.10
90	4.9	5.24	5.47	5.41	3.52	4.13	4.96	4.20	4.07	4.50	4.01
95	3.7	3.97	4.30	4.58	2.43	2.74	3.71	3.09	3.18	3.45	3.15
100	2.8	2.97	3.69	4.20	1.91	1.94	2.70	2.04	2.23	2.39	2.49

[1]For 1939–41 and 1949–51, data shown are for the entire nonwhite population. During these periods, life tables were not constructed for the black population. See Technical notes.

Table 12. Estimated life expectancy at birth in years, by race and sex: Death-registration States, 1900–28, and United States, 1929–98

[For selected years, life table values shown are estimates; see Technical notes. Beginning 1970 excludes deaths of nonresidents of the United States; see Technical notes]

Area and year	All races Both sexes	All races Male	All races Female	White Both sexes	White Male	White Female	Black[4] Both sexes	Black[4] Male	Black[4] Female
United States[1]									
1998.	76.7	73.8	79.5	77.3	74.5	80.0	71.3	67.6	74.8
1997.	76.5	73.6	79.4	77.2	74.3	79.9	71.1	67.2	74.7
1996.	76.1	73.1	79.1	76.8	73.9	79.7	70.2	66.1	74.2
1995.	75.8	72.5	78.9	76.5	73.4	79.6	69.6	65.2	73.9
1994.	75.7	72.4	79.0	76.5	73.3	79.6	69.5	64.9	73.9
1993.	75.5	72.2	78.8	76.3	73.1	79.5	69.2	64.6	73.7
1992.	75.8	72.3	79.1	76.5	73.2	79.8	69.6	65.0	73.9
1991.	75.5	72.0	78.9	76.3	72.9	79.6	69.3	64.6	73.8
1990.	75.4	71.8	78.8	76.1	72.7	79.4	69.1	64.5	73.6
1989.	75.1	71.7	78.5	75.9	72.5	79.2	68.8	64.3	73.3
1988.	74.9	71.4	78.3	75.6	72.2	78.9	68.9	64.4	73.2
1987.	74.9	71.4	78.3	75.6	72.1	78.9	69.1	64.7	73.4
1986.	74.7	71.2	78.2	75.4	71.9	78.8	69.1	64.8	73.4
1985.	74.7	71.1	78.2	75.3	71.8	78.7	69.3	65.0	73.4
1984.	74.7	71.1	78.2	75.3	71.8	78.7	69.5	65.3	73.6
1983.	74.6	71.0	78.1	75.2	71.6	78.7	69.4	65.2	73.5
1982.	74.5	70.8	78.1	75.1	71.5	78.7	69.4	65.1	73.6
1981.	74.1	70.4	77.8	74.8	71.1	78.4	68.9	64.5	73.2
1980.	73.7	70.0	77.4	74.4	70.7	78.1	68.1	63.8	72.5
1979.	73.9	70.0	77.8	74.6	70.8	78.4	68.5	64.0	72.9
1978.	73.5	69.6	77.3	74.1	70.4	78.0	68.1	63.7	72.4
1977.	73.3	69.5	77.2	74.0	70.2	77.9	67.7	63.4	72.0
1976.	72.9	69.1	76.8	73.6	69.9	77.5	67.2	62.9	71.6
1975.	72.6	68.8	76.6	73.4	69.5	77.3	66.8	62.4	71.3
1974.	72.0	68.2	75.9	72.8	69.0	76.7	66.0	61.7	70.3
1973.	71.4	67.6	75.3	72.2	68.5	76.1	65.0	60.9	69.3
1972[2]	71.2	67.4	75.1	72.0	68.3	75.9	64.7	60.4	69.1
1971.	71.1	67.4	75.0	72.0	68.3	75.8	64.6	60.5	68.9
1970.	70.8	67.1	74.7	71.7	68.0	75.6	64.1	60.0	68.3
1969.	70.5	66.8	74.4	71.4	67.7	75.3	64.5	60.6	68.6
1968.	70.2	66.6	74.1	71.1	67.5	75.0	64.1	60.4	67.9
1967.	70.5	67.0	74.3	71.4	67.8	75.2	64.9	61.4	68.5
1966.	70.2	66.7	73.9	71.1	67.5	74.8	64.2	60.9	67.6
1965.	70.2	66.8	73.8	71.1	67.6	74.8	64.3	61.2	67.6
1964.	70.2	66.8	73.7	71.0	67.7	74.7	64.2	61.3	67.3
1963[3]	69.9	66.6	73.4	70.8	67.4	74.4	63.7	61.0	66.6
1962[3]	70.1	66.9	73.5	70.9	67.7	74.5	64.2	61.6	66.9
1961.	70.2	67.1	73.6	71.0	67.8	74.6	64.5	62.0	67.1
1960.	69.7	66.6	73.1	70.6	67.4	74.1	63.6	61.1	66.3
1959.	69.9	66.8	73.2	70.7	67.5	74.2	63.9	61.3	66.5
1958.	69.6	66.6	72.9	70.5	67.4	73.9	63.4	61.0	65.8
1957.	69.5	66.4	72.7	70.3	67.2	73.7	63.0	60.7	65.5
1956.	69.7	66.7	72.9	70.5	67.5	73.9	63.6	61.3	66.1
1955.	69.6	66.7	72.8	70.5	67.4	73.7	63.7	61.4	66.1
1954.	69.6	66.7	72.8	70.5	67.5	73.7	63.4	61.1	65.9
1953.	68.8	66.0	72.0	69.7	66.8	73.0	62.0	59.7	64.5
1952.	68.6	65.8	71.6	69.5	66.6	72.6	61.4	59.1	63.8
1951.	68.4	65.6	71.4	69.3	66.5	72.4	61.2	59.2	63.4
1950.	68.2	65.6	71.1	69.1	66.5	72.2	60.8	59.1	62.9
1949.	68.0	65.2	70.7	68.8	66.2	71.9	60.6	58.9	62.7
1948.	67.2	64.6	69.9	68.0	65.5	71.0	60.0	58.1	62.5
1947.	66.8	64.4	69.7	67.6	65.2	70.5	59.7	57.9	61.9
1946.	66.7	64.4	69.4	67.5	65.1	70.3	59.1	57.5	61.0
1945.	65.9	63.6	67.9	66.8	64.4	69.5	57.7	56.1	59.6
1944.	65.2	63.6	66.8	66.2	64.5	68.4	56.6	55.8	57.7
1943.	63.3	62.4	64.4	64.2	63.2	65.7	55.6	55.4	56.1
1942.	66.2	64.7	67.9	67.3	65.9	69.4	56.6	55.4	58.2
1941.	64.8	63.1	66.8	66.2	64.4	68.5	53.8	52.5	55.3
1940.	62.9	60.8	65.2	64.2	62.1	66.6	53.1	51.5	54.9
1939.	63.7	62.1	65.4	64.9	63.3	66.6	54.5	53.2	56.0
1938.	63.5	61.9	65.3	65.0	63.2	66.8	52.9	51.7	54.3
1937.	60.0	58.0	62.4	61.4	59.3	63.8	50.3	48.3	52.5
1936.	58.5	56.6	60.6	59.8	58.0	61.9	49.0	47.0	51.4

See footnotes at end of table.

Table 12. Estimated life expectancy at birth in years, by race and sex: Death-registration States, 1900–28, and United States, 1929–98—Con.

[For selected years, life table values shown are estimates; see Technical notes. Beginning 1970 excludes deaths of nonresidents of the United States; see Technical notes]

Area and year	All races Both sexes	Male	Female	White Both sexes	Male	Female	Black[4] Both sexes	Male	Female
United States—Con.									
1935.	61.7	59.9	63.9	62.9	61.0	65.0	53.1	51.3	55.2
1934.	61.1	59.3	63.3	62.4	60.5	64.6	51.8	50.2	53.7
1933.	63.3	61.7	65.1	64.3	62.7	66.3	54.7	53.5	56.0
1932.	62.1	61.0	63.5	63.2	62.0	64.5	53.7	52.8	54.6
1931.	61.1	59.4	63.1	62.6	60.8	64.7	50.4	49.5	51.5
1930.	59.7	58.1	61.6	61.4	59.7	63.5	48.1	47.3	49.2
1929.	57.1	55.8	58.7	58.6	57.2	60.3	46.7	45.7	47.8
Death-registration States									
1928.	56.8	55.6	58.3	58.4	57.0	60.0	46.3	45.6	47.0
1927.	60.4	59.0	62.1	62.0	60.5	63.9	48.2	47.6	48.9
1926.	56.7	55.5	58.0	58.2	57.0	59.6	44.6	43.7	45.6
1925.	59.0	57.6	60.6	60.7	59.3	62.4	45.7	44.9	46.7
1924.	59.7	58.1	61.5	61.4	59.8	63.4	46.6	45.5	47.8
1923.	57.2	56.1	58.5	58.3	57.1	59.6	48.3	47.7	48.9
1922.	59.6	58.4	61.0	60.4	59.1	61.9	52.4	51.8	53.0
1921.	60.8	60.0	61.8	61.8	60.8	62.9	51.5	51.6	51.3
1920.	54.1	53.6	54.6	54.9	54.4	55.6	45.3	45.5	45.2
1919.	54.7	53.5	56.0	55.8	54.5	57.4	44.5	44.5	44.4
1918.	39.1	36.6	42.2	39.8	37.1	43.2	31.1	29.9	32.5
1917.	50.9	48.4	54.0	52.0	49.3	55.3	38.8	37.0	40.8
1916.	51.7	49.6	54.3	52.5	50.2	55.2	41.3	39.6	43.1
1915.	54.5	52.5	56.8	55.1	53.1	57.5	38.9	37.5	40.5
1914.	54.2	52.0	56.8	54.9	52.7	57.5	38.9	37.1	40.8
1913.	52.5	50.3	55.0	53.0	50.8	55.7	38.4	36.7	40.3
1912.	53.5	51.5	55.9	53.9	51.9	56.2	37.9	35.9	40.0
1911.	52.6	50.9	54.4	53.0	51.3	54.9	36.4	34.6	38.2
1910.	50.0	48.4	51.8	50.3	48.6	52.0	35.6	33.8	37.5
1909.	52.1	50.5	53.8	52.5	50.9	54.2	35.7	34.2	37.3
1908.	51.1	49.5	52.8	51.5	49.9	53.3	34.9	33.8	36.0
1907.	47.6	45.6	49.9	48.1	46.0	50.4	32.5	31.1	34.0
1906.	48.7	46.9	50.8	49.3	47.3	51.4	32.9	31.8	33.9
1905.	48.7	47.3	50.2	49.1	47.6	50.6	31.3	29.6	33.1
1904.	47.6	46.2	49.1	48.0	46.6	49.5	30.8	29.1	32.7
1903.	50.5	49.1	52.0	50.9	49.5	52.5	33.1	31.7	34.6
1902.	51.5	49.8	53.4	51.9	50.2	53.8	34.6	32.9	36.4
1901.	49.1	47.6	50.6	49.4	48.0	51.0	33.7	32.2	35.3
1900.	47.3	46.3	48.3	47.6	46.6	48.7	33.0	32.5	33.5

[1]Alaska included in 1959 and Hawaii in 1960.
[2]Deaths based on a 50-percent sample.
[3]Figures by race exclude data for residents of New Jersey; see Technical notes.
[4]Prior to 1970, data for the black population are not available. Data shown for 1900–69 are for the nonwhite population. See Technical notes.

Technical notes

The life table program—Three series of complete life tables are prepared by the National Center for Health Statistics for the U.S. population—decennial, annual preliminary, and annual final. The U.S. decennial life tables are based on decennial census data and deaths for a 3-year period around the census year. Preliminary life tables are based on a substantial sample (approximately 90 percent) of death records. Estimates of life expectancy from the preliminary series are published annually. The annual final life tables (referred to in this section as "annual life tables") are based on a complete count of all reported deaths.

Available since 1945, the annual life tables are based on deaths occurring during the calendar year and on midyear postcensal population estimates provided by the U.S. Bureau of the Census. From 1945 to 1996, the annual life tables were abridged life tables and were constructed by reference to a standard table (3). Beginning with 1997 mortality data, complete life tables are constructed using a new methodology (4, 5). Also for 1997, life expectancy and other life table values were shown for ages 85 to 100 for the first time as part of the annual U.S. life tables. Previously, the annual life tables were closed at age 85 years. Extension of the oldest age interval was implemented by NCHS for several reasons: survival in the United States is such that approximately one-third of the population survives beyond age 85; improvements have occurred in age reporting at older ages; and high-quality old-age mortality data are available from the Medicare program.

Geographic coverage—The geographic areas covered in life tables before 1929–31 were limited to the death-registration areas. Life tables for 1900–1902 and 1909–11 were constructed using mortality data from the 1900 death-registration States (10 States and the District of Columbia) and for 1919–21 from the 1920 death-registration States (34 States and the District of Columbia). The tables for 1929–31 through 1958 cover the conterminous United States. Decennial life table values for the 3-year period 1959–61 were derived from data that include both Alaska and Hawaii for each year (tables 10 and 11). Data for each year shown in table 12 include Alaska beginning in 1959 and Hawaii beginning in 1960. However, it is not believed that the inclusion of these two States materially affects life table values.

Revised life table values, 1961–89—Life table values for 1960–69, 1970–79, and 1980–89 were constructed using the U.S. decennial life tables for 1959–61, 1969–71, and 1979–81, respectively, as the standard tables. The life table values for years prior to 1989 appearing in this publication are based on revised intercensal estimates of the populations for those years. As a result, the life table values for these years may differ from the life table values for those years published in *Vital Statistics of the United States* for 1989 and earlier years. Life table values for 1991 and later are based on postcensal population estimates and will be recalculated when intercensal estimates become available.

New Jersey data, 1962–64—The life tables for 1962 and 1963 for the six population groups involving race do not include data from New Jersey, which omitted the item on race from its certificates of live birth, death, and fetal death in use at the beginning of 1962. The item was restored during the latter part of 1962. However, the certificate revision without this item was used for most of 1962 as well as for 1963. For computing vital rates, populations by age, race, and sex (excluding New Jersey) were estimated to obtain comparable denominators. Approximately 7 percent of the New Jersey death records for 1964 did not contain the race designation. When the records were being electronically processed for this State, the "race not stated" deaths were proportionally allocated to white or to black.

Nonresidents—Beginning in 1970, the deaths of nonresidents of the United States have been excluded from the life table statistics.

Estimation of life table functions—For some years, it was necessary to estimate life table functions for some race-sex groups. In tables 10 and 11, figures for the black population during the periods 1949–51 and 1959–61 were estimated using figures for the nonwhite population. Life table functions were also missing in tables 10 and 11 for race-sex groups for the periods from 1900–1902 to 1939–41. Figures were missing for the following groups:

Years	Race and sex
1900–1902	Total white, total black
1909–11	Total white, total black
1919–21	Total, male, female, total white, total black
1929–31	Total, male, female, total white, total black

These figures were estimated by weighted averages using population distributions as the weights. For example, life expectancy at age 20 years for the total black population was estimated by a weighted average of black male and black female life expectancies at age 20, using as weights the population distribution by sex of the black population age 20 years.

Annual life tables were initiated in 1945 for white males, white females, all other males, and all other females. The figures in table 12 by race and sex for the following years were estimated using a procedure other than the abridged life table methodology (11).

Years	Race and sex
1900–45	Total
1900–47	Male
1900–47	Female
1900–50	White
1900–44	White male
1900–44	White female

Annual life table functions were not calculated for the black population prior to 1970. In table 12, life expectancy for the black population for years prior to 1970 are estimated using figures for the total nonwhite population.

Population bases for computing life tables—The population used for computing life table values shown in this section (furnished by the U.S. Bureau of the Census) represents the resident population of the United States. The age-specific populations used for computing the 1998 life table values are based on the July 1, 1998, population estimates that are consistent with the 1990 Census (12). The 1990 Census counts by race and age were modified. Race was modified to be consistent with the Office of Management and Budget categories and historical categories for mortality data. The modification procedures for race and age are described in a census report (13).

Medicare data—Death rates at the oldest ages based on Medicare data are known to be more accurate than those based on vital statistics and census data. Consequently, q_x values calculated for ages 85 to 99 years are based on Medicare data prepared by the Health Care Financing Administration (HCFA). Medicare data were limited to the group insured for hospital insurance as age reporting is considered best among this group (5, 9, 10). For the 1998 life tables, 1997 Medicare data was used because 1998 data were not available in time for the preparation of this report.

Methodology

A more detailed treatment of the methodology used to calculate these life tables is contained in a separate report (4). Calculation of the complete life table is derived from the probability of death (q_x), which depends on the number of deaths (D_x) and the midyear population (P_x) for each single year of age (x) observed during the calendar year of interest.

Adjustment for deaths for which age was not reported—An adjustment must be made to account for the small proportion of deaths each year for which age is not reported. The data are aggregated into 5-year age groups for those aged 5 years and over and into single years of age for those under 5 years. The number of deaths in each age category is adjusted proportionally to account for those with not-stated ages. The following factor is used to make the adjustment. This factor (F) is calculated for each race-sex group for which life tables are constructed.

$$F = \frac{D}{D^a} \tag{1}$$

where D is the total number of deaths and D^a is the total number of deaths for which age is stated. F is then applied by multiplying it times the number of deaths in each age group. Table I shows values for F by race and sex used to adjust the 1998 mortality data.

Interpolation of P_x and D_x—Anomalies, both random and those associated with reporting age at death, can be problematic when using vital statistics and census data by single years of age to estimate the probability of death (1). Graduation techniques are often used to eliminate these anomalies and to derive a smooth curve by age. Beer's ordinary minimized fifth difference formula is used to obtain smoothed values of P_x and D_x (see reference 4 for details on the application of Beer's method).

Calculation of q_0—q_0 is calculated by using a birth cohort method employing a separation factor (f) defined as the proportion of infant deaths in year t occurring to infants born in the previous year ($t-1$). f can be calculated by categorizing infant deaths by date of birth. The probability of death in the first year is calculated as

$$q_0 = \frac{D_0 (1-f)}{B^t} + \frac{D_0 f}{B^{t-1}} \tag{2}$$

Table I. Values for F used to adjust for not-stated age based on 1998 mortality data

Race and sex	Total deaths	Total deaths for which age was not stated	F
Total	2,337,256	411	1.00017588
Male	1,157,260	324	1.00028005
Female	1,179,996	87	1.00007373
White	2,015,984	310	1.00015379
Male	990,190	251	1.00025355
Female	1,025,794	59	1.00005752
Black	278,440	93	1.00033412
Male	143,417	67	1.00046739
Female	135,023	26	1.00019260

where D_0 is the number of infant deaths adjusted for not-reported age, and B^t and B^{t-1} are the numbers of births in years t and t-1, respectively. Table II shows separation factors and numbers of births by race and sex for 1997–98.

Calculation of q_x for ages 1–84 years—q_x is calculated assuming that l_x (number of survivors at exact age x in the life table population) declines linearly between x and x+1, i.e., that deaths between exact age x and x+1 occur on average at age x+½. This simplification is generally considered acceptable when age intervals are 1 year of age in length (1). Under this assumption, $l_x = L_x + \frac{1}{2}d_x$ where L_x is the average life table population at risk of dying between ages x and x+1 and d_x is the number of deaths occurring between age x and x+1. q_x is then

$$q_x = \frac{d_x}{l_x} = \frac{d_x}{L_x + \frac{1}{2} d_x}$$

One can make the same assumption for the observed population, i.e., that the observed population aged x at risk of dying at the beginning of the year (N_x) declines linearly between ages x and x+1. Under this assumption, $N_x = P_x + \frac{1}{2}D_x$ where P_x is the midyear population or average observed population at risk of dying between ages x and x+1 and D_x is the observed number of deaths occurring between ages x and x+1. q_x is calculated as

$$q_x = \frac{D_x}{N_x} = \frac{D_x}{P_x + \frac{1}{2} D_x} \tag{3}$$

For $x = 1$ to 4, D_x is the observed number of deaths adjusted for not-stated age and P_x is obtained by Beer's interpolation formula. For $x = 5$ to 84, both D_x and P_x are obtained by interpolation (4).

Use of Medicare data at ages 85 to 99—There is ample evidence that the rate of increase in q_x declines above age 85 years (4, 10, 14, 15, and 16). The change in q_x for ages over 85 years can be expressed using the formula

$$q_x = q_{x-1} \cdot e^{k_x} \tag{4}$$

where k_x denotes the age-specific rate of mortality change with age (10,15). Solving for k_x gives

$$k_x = \ln(q_x) - \ln(q_{x-1}) \tag{5}$$

Values for k_x are then obtained from the Medicare data. Table III shows values for k by age, race, and sex based on 1997 Medicare data. These data show clearly a declining rate of increase in q_x above age 85 years. These k_x values are then used to obtain q_x values for ages 85 to 99 using equation 4. This method allows for flexibility in cases where the Medicare data are not available in a timely fashion. In these cases, Medicare data for the previous year can be used to calculate k_x values. Finally, $_\infty q_{100}$ is set equal to 1.0 since all will die at some point in this open-ended age interval. Once q_x is obtained for each single year of age, the other life table functions may be easily calculated.

Survivor function (l_x)—The life table radix, l_0, is set at 100,000. For ages greater than 0, the number of survivors remaining at exact age x is calculated as

$$l_x = l_{x-1} (1 - q_{x-1}) \tag{6}$$

Decrement function (d_x)—The number of deaths occurring between age x and $x + 1$ is calculated from the survivor function.

$$d_x = l_x - l_{x+1} = l_x \, q_x \tag{7}$$

Note that $_\infty d_{100} = {}_\infty l_{100}$ since $_\infty q_{100} = 1.0$.

Table II. Births in 1997 and 1998, deaths in 1998 of infants born in 1997 and 1998, and separation factors by race and sex: United States

	Total			White			Black		
	Both sexes	Male	Female	Both sexes	Male	Female	Both sexes	Male	Female
Births									
1997.	3,880,894	1,985,596	1,895,298	3,072,640	1,573,622	1,499,018	599,913	304,530	295,383
1998.	3,941,553	2,016,205	1,925,348	3,118,727	1,596,704	1,522,023	609,902	310,107	299,795
Deaths in 1998 of infants born in									
1997.	3,573	2,010	1,563	2,332	1,329	1,003	1,080	596	484
1998.	24,748	13,748	11,000	16,199	8,981	7,218	7,626	4,276	3,350
Separation factor	0.126	0.128	0.124	0.126	0.129	0.122	0.124	0.122	0.126

Table III. k values by age, race, and sex based on insured Medicare data: United States, 1997

	Total			White			Black		
Age	Both sexes	Male	Female	Both sexes	Male	Female	Both sexes	Male	Female
84–85	0.092590	0.089728	0.103281	0.093742	0.09136	0.10428	0.071864	0.066047	0.082589
85–86	0.090210	0.087018	0.100251	0.091842	0.08897	0.10185	0.070794	0.064457	0.081079
86–87	0.087830	0.084308	0.097221	0.089942	0.08658	0.09942	0.069724	0.062867	0.079569
87–88	0.085450	0.081598	0.094191	0.088042	0.08419	0.09699	0.068654	0.061277	0.078059
88–89	0.083070	0.078888	0.091161	0.086142	0.08180	0.09456	0.067584	0.059687	0.076549
89–90	0.080690	0.076178	0.088131	0.084242	0.07941	0.09213	0.066514	0.058097	0.075039
90–91	0.078310	0.073468	0.085101	0.082342	0.07702	0.08970	0.065444	0.056507	0.073529
91–92	0.075930	0.070758	0.082071	0.080442	0.07463	0.08727	0.064374	0.054917	0.072019
92–93	0.073550	0.068048	0.079041	0.078542	0.07224	0.08484	0.063304	0.053327	0.070509
93–94	0.071170	0.065338	0.076011	0.076642	0.06985	0.08241	0.062234	0.051737	0.068999
94–95	0.068790	0.062628	0.072981	0.074742	0.06746	0.07998	0.061164	0.050147	0.067489
95–96	0.066410	0.059918	0.069951	0.072842	0.06507	0.07755	0.060094	0.048557	0.065979
96–97	0.064030	0.057208	0.066921	0.070942	0.06268	0.07512	0.059024	0.046967	0.064469
97–98	0.061650	0.054498	0.063891	0.069042	0.06029	0.07269	0.057954	0.045377	0.062959
98–99	0.059270	0.051788	0.060861	0.067142	0.05790	0.07026	0.056884	0.043787	0.061449

Stationary population (L_x)—The stationary population at ages 1 to 99 years is calculated assuming that the survivor function declines linearly between age x and $x + 1$. This gives the formula

$$L_x = \tfrac{1}{2}(l_x + l_{x+1}) = l_x - \tfrac{1}{2}d_x \qquad [8]$$

For $x = 0$, the separation factor f is used to calculate L_0.

$$L_0 = f\,l_0 + (1 - f)\,l_1$$

$_\infty L_{100}$ is calculated by surviving the life table cohort from age 100 using equations 4, 5, and 6 until L_x at these ages is essentially zero (somewhere between ages 110 and 120). q_x for these ages can be extrapolated from the Medicare data using equation 4. However, k_x values must be estimated for these ages. k_x can be modeled as a linear function of age

$$k_x = k_{85} + (x - 85)s \qquad [9]$$

where s is the slope of the change in k_x by age and k_{85} is calculated as $[\ln(q_{88}/q_{81})]/7$ in order to minimize the effects of random fluctuations (10, 16). s can be obtained by treating equation 9 as a linear regression model. Calculated values for s are shown in table IV. The predicted values for k_x are then used to calculate q_x above age 100 using equation 4. The corresponding L_x values for ages 100 years and over are then summed to give $_\infty L_{100}$.

Person-years lived at and above age x (T_x)—T_x is calculated by summing L_x values at and above age x.

$$T_x = \sum_{t=0}^{\infty} L_{x+t} \qquad [10]$$

Life expectancy at age x (e_x)—Life expectancy at exact age x is calculated as

$$e_x = \frac{T_x}{l_x} \qquad [11]$$

Table IV. Slope of the change in k values (s) by age, race, and sex

Race and sex	s
Total, both sexes	−0.002379
Male	−0.002710
Female	−0.003031
White, both sexes	−0.001902
Male	−0.002390
Female	−0.002427
Black, both sexes	−0.001074
Male	−0.001586
Female	−0.001512

Abridging the Complete Life Table

An abridged or collapsed version of the complete life table can be easily calculated in which life table functions are shown for 5-year rather than single-year age intervals. It is often desirable to summarize the life table and save space when publishing life table data by single years of age is unnecessary (17). The abridgement of the complete life table is simplified by an important property of three of the six life table functions. The l_x, T_x, and e_x functions describe exact age x, i.e., the beginning of the age interval x to $x+n$ (n denotes the length of the age interval for 5-year age intervals $n = 5$). Life expectancy at age 20 (e_{20}), for example, has the same value regardless of whether the age interval is 20–21 years or 20–25 years. Thus, the values l_x, T_x, and e_x can be extracted at 5-year intervals from the complete life table and placed into the abridged life table (compare l_x, T_x, and e_x in table V with the same functions in table 1). It is also illustrative to compare values for e_x and l_x in tables A and B with their corresponding values presented in tables 1–9. The q_x, d_x, and L_x functions, in contrast, describe the age interval x to $x+n$. In fact, for abridged life tables, the notation for these functions is different ($_nq_x$, $_nd_x$, $_nL_x$). Thus, $_5q_{20}$ is the probability of dying between ages 20 and 25 years and will obviously be somewhat larger than q_{20}, the probability of dying between ages 20 and 21 years. Taking this into account, $_nq_x$, $_nd_x$, and $_nL_x$ must be recalculated in the abridged life table. It is simplest to begin with $_nd_x$. The calculations are made for all but the final age interval as follows:

$$_nd_x = l_x - l_{x+n}$$

$$_nq_x = \frac{_nd_x}{l_x}$$

$$_nL_x = T_x - T_{x+n}$$

Note that for the open-ended interval, ages 100 and over: $_\infty d_{100} = l_{100}$, $_\infty q_{100} = 1.0$, and $_\infty L_{100} = T_{100}$.

Table V shows each of the life table functions for the 1998 U.S. total population abridged from table 1.

Table V. Abridged life table for the total population: United States, 1998

Age	Proportion dying during age interval q_x	Number living at beginning of age interval l_x	Number dying during age interval d_x	Stationary population in the age interval L_x	Stationary population in this and all subsequent age intervals T_x	Life expectancy at beginning of age interval e_x
0–1	0.00721	100,000	721	99,370	7,671,400	76.7
1–5	0.00139	99,279	138	396,786	7,572,030	76.3
5–10	0.00089	99,141	88	495,473	7,175,244	72.4
10–15	0.00110	99,053	109	495,057	6,679,771	67.4
15–20	0.00353	98,944	349	493,926	6,184,714	62.5
20–25	0.00476	98,595	469	491,820	5,690,788	57.7
25–30	0.00487	98,126	478	489,450	5,198,968	53.0
30–35	0.00600	97,648	586	486,840	4,709,518	48.2
35–40	0.00819	97,062	795	483,428	4,222,678	43.5
40–45	0.01176	96,267	1,132	478,670	3,739,250	38.8
45–50	0.01728	95,135	1,644	471,811	3,260,580	34.3
50–55	0.02564	93,491	2,397	461,839	2,788,769	29.8
55–60	0.04009	91,094	3,652	446,966	2,326,930	25.5
60–65	0.06302	87,442	5,511	424,280	1,879,964	21.5
65–70	0.09437	81,931	7,732	391,364	1,455,684	17.8
70–75	0.14239	74,199	10,565	345,660	1,064,320	14.3
75–80	0.20604	63,634	13,111	286,484	718,660	11.3
80–85	0.31641	50,523	15,986	213,526	432,176	8.6
85–90	0.46104	34,537	15,923	131,897	218,650	6.3
90–95	0.61502	18,614	11,448	62,020	86,753	4.7
95–100	0.75426	7,166	5,405	20,150	24,733	3.5
100+	1.00000	1,761	1,761	4,583	4,583	2.6

Contents

Abstract 1
Introduction 1
Data and methods 1
   Explanation of the columns of the life table 2
Results 3
   Life expectancy in the United States 3
   Survivorship in the United States. 4
References 5
List of detailed tables 6
Technical notes 35

This document is hereby certified as an official Federal document and is fully admissible as evidence in Federal court. Under Federal Rule of Evidence 902: "Self-authentication," (FED.R.EVID.902), no extrinsic evidence of authenticity, that is, seal or stamp, is required as a condition for admissibility of this document as evidence in court.

Suggested citation

Anderson RN. United States life tables, 1998. National vital statistics reports; vol 48 no. 18. Hyattsville, Maryland: National Center for Health Statistics. 2001.

National Center for Health Statistics

Director, Edward J. Sondik, Ph.D.
Deputy Director, Jack R. Anderson

Division of Vital Statistics

Director, Mary Anne Freedman

To receive this publication regularly, contact the National Center for Health Statistics by calling 301-458-4636. E-mail: nchsquery@cdc.gov
Internet: www.cdc.gov/nchs/

U.S. DEPARTMENT OF
HEALTH & HUMAN SERVICES

Centers for Disease Control and Prevention
National Center for Health Statistics
6525 Belcrest Road
Hyattsville, Maryland 20782-2003

DHHS Publication No. (PHS) 2001–1120
1-0093 (2/01)

OFFICIAL BUSINESS
PENALTY FOR PRIVATE USE, $300

FIRST CLASS MAIL
POSTAGE & FEES PAID
CDC/NCHS
PERMIT NO. G-284

www.ingramcontent.com/pod-product-compliance
Lightning Source LLC
Chambersburg PA
CBHW080932290526
45795CB00007BA/2715